MAKING SENSE
OF LIFE STAGES,
THE WORKPLACE
AND TMI

MAKING SENSE

OF LIFE STAGES,

THE WORKPLACE

AND TMI

(Too Much Information)

Cynthia C. J. Shoemaker, Ph.D.

To order additional copies of this book, contact:
Xlibris
1-888-795-4274
www.Xlibris.com
Orders@Xlibris.com
595160

Contents

Making Sense of Your World, Life Stages and TMI (Too Much Information)

Chapter 1   Dealing with Chaos and Information Overload 9
Chapter 2   TMI and Chaos in the Corporate World 17
Chapter 3   The U.S. Military Services: Making Sense
              in Leadership Shifting from the Industrial Age
              to the Information Age with Complexity Leadership 25
Chapter 4   Make Sense in Government Agencies:
              IT with Too Much Information and Chaos............................ 33

Making Sense of Life Stages and TMI

Chapter 5   Making Sense of Too Much Information (TMI)
              in the Mid-Twenties 39
Chapter 6   TMI Around Ages 13 to 15 1/2 Years of Age...................... 45
Chapter 7   TMI and the Nine to Eleven Year Old 55
Chapter 8   TMI at Two and a Half Years Old Up to Four Years Old 59
Chapter 9   Making Sense in Your Life: When Serious Illness
              strikes a Family Member... 65
Chapter 10   Reinventing Yourself at Any Life Stage
              and Planning for Later Years....................................... 69

Conclusion... 73
References 75

List of Figures

Figure 1.1   Making Sense of Your World and Your Stage of Life............... 8
Figure 1.2   Foresight Diamond... 13
Figure 2.1   Sensemaking Model: Making Sense of the Corporate World.......16
Figure 2.2   Knowledge Cycle 22
Figure 3.1   Making Sense of Your World and the U.S. Military
             Transition Steps: Sensemaking in the Knowledge Era.......... 24
Figure 3.2   Foresight Diamond: Helps in Making Sense Strategically 28
Figure 3.3   More Detailed Version of Foresight Diamond........................ 29
Figure 3.4   Thinking Through and Seeing 30
Figure 4.1   Making Sense of Your World, Your Life and Your Work:
             Sensemaking Model—Government Agencies Moving
             into the Information Age/Knowledge Era 32
Figure 5.1   Making Sense of Your World and Your Stage of Life:
             Sensemaking Model—Mid-Twenties Age Group 38
Figure 6.1   Making Sense of Your World and Your Stage of Life:
             Sensemaking Model—13 to 15 ½ Years of Age.................... 44
Figure 6.2   Laugh and the world laughs with you 48
Figure 6.3   Begin at the beginning . . . hope.. 51
Figure 6.4   Hope whispers try it one more time...................................... 52
Figure 6.5   Don't listen.. 53
Figure 7.1   Making Sense of Your World and Stages of Life:
             Sensemaking Model—9 to 11 Years of Age......................... 54
Figure 7.2   "If I Were in Charge of the World" 56
Figure 8.1   Making Sense of Your World and Stages of Life:
             Sensemaking Model—Ages 2 ½ to 4 years of Age 58
Figure 9.1   Making Sense of My World and My Life:
             When Serious Illness Strikes Someone Close....................... 64
Figure 10.1 Making Sense of Your World and Your Stage of Life:
             Sensemaking Model—Senior Retirement Planning............... 68

Graphics credits: Collage graphics Figures 6.2, 6.3, 6.4, 6.5 by Madison A. Jones; Figure 7.2 by Beverly J. Lundeen.

Making Sense of Your World, Life Stages and TMI

(Too Much Information)

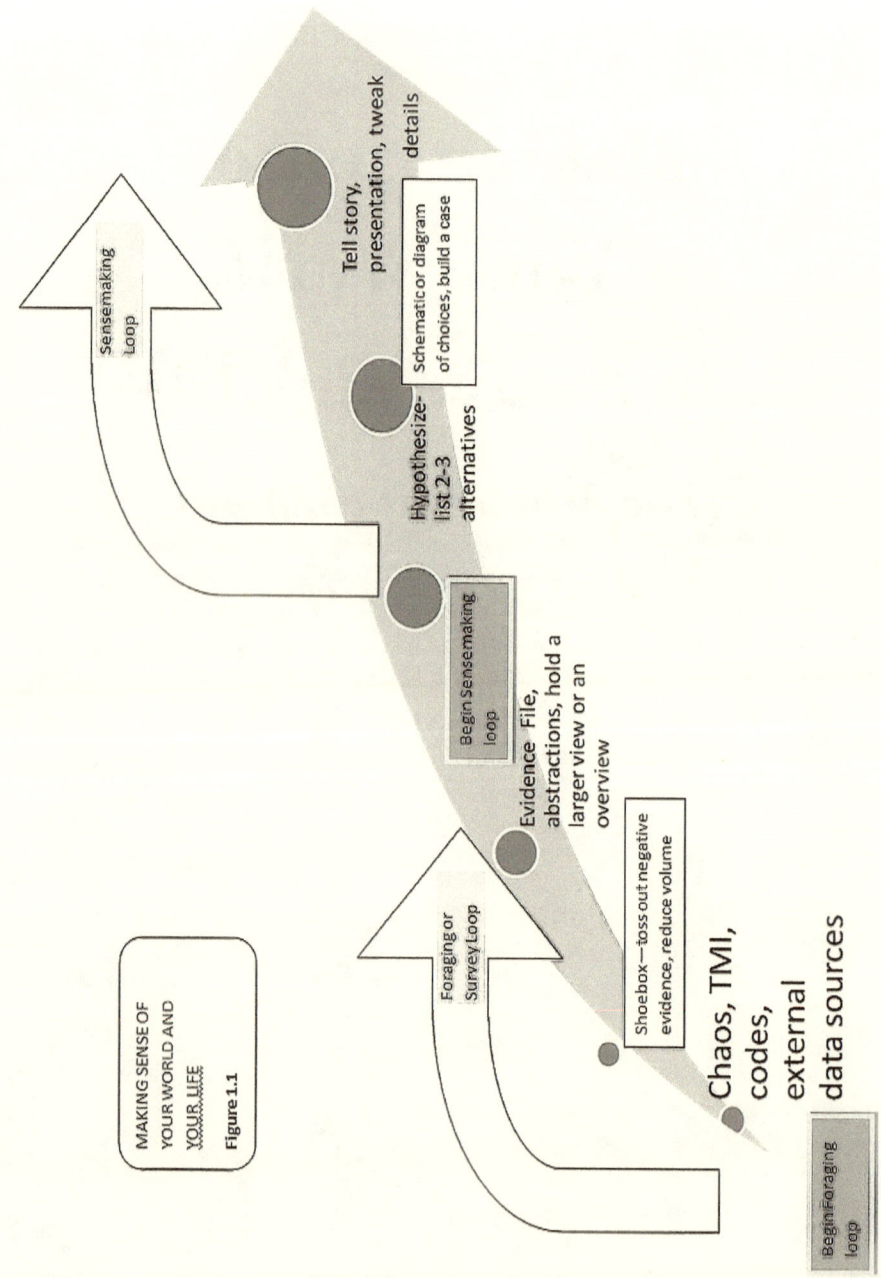

MAKING SENSE OF
YOUR WORLD AND
YOUR LIFE

Figure 1.1

Sensemaking
Loop

Tell story,
presentation, tweak
details

Schematic or diagram
of choices, build a case

Hypothesize-
list 2-3
alternatives

Begin Sensemaking
loop

Evidence File,
abstractions, hold a
larger view or an
overview

Foraging or
Survey Loop

Shoebox—toss out negative
evidence, reduce volume

Chaos, TMI,
codes,
external
data sources

Begin Foraging
loop

Chapter 1

Dealing with Chaos and Information Overload

Applying insights to wider circumstances and life stages sometimes can give one a new and diversified set of behaviors and strategies as one goes through different periods of life. *Seeing* codes or "codification", unspoken rules and conventions around one can help one to move forward in new ways. This book applies a variety of sensemaking theories to the various complexities that surround life and especially life in the Knowledge Era or Information Age. With Internet, social networking and new information technology emerging all the time, the "information space" surrounding life events and life stages can lead to feelings of chaos. The required complexities needed to sort and make sense of events can feel overwhelming and even chaotic to individuals and to corporations and other enterprises.

Some life events are those one is born into, such as being physically challenged or being a female in a rural area; some are grown into, such as being a 'tweenager' (ages 11-14); being in the middle twenties; or approaching retirement at any age. However some life events are thrust upon us such as a death or serious illness, or unexpected divorce.

Any of these stages or events can produce what feels like vast amounts of information and 'codes' of how one is "supposed" to feel or proceed. If one works in a highly codified workplace such as the Navy or a civilian government agency with new initiatives; or one's cultural and/or geographic region has "codes" about next steps and feelings, one can feel like one is swimming upstream. One employee in a military service was told "don't make waves" when she had new ideas or suggestions for innovative practices. The Complexity Leadership approach of encouraging "learn, innovate, and adapt" was missing! Another person in a different smaller segment of the same military service was able to change trucks running at a '35% fill-capacity' to requiring an '85% fill-capacity' by changing the timing on the long-accepted-and-old (dating from less expensive gas prices) schedule metric and thus actually saved a billion dollars. (D. Moore, Oct. 2012). New ideas and fresh insights can be helpful to the budget as well as to individuals.

Applying innovation research to human development, in Part II "Sensemaking in Your Life" reveals insights as technology can make things confusing with "too much information (TMI)". Think of a two-and-a-half-year-old child told to be a "big girl" (or "big boy"). The child isn't sure what a "big girl/boy" is, but is sure he/she doesn't know how. So the child clings to wearing diapers and refusing to be toilet trained or to another babyish behavior.

Similarly an 11 ½ year old who is growing fast, receives TMI (Too Much Information) about what it means to be tweenager from movies, TV shows, video games, hand held electronics, friends and even from books. They feel stretched and overwhelmed and sometimes just blow up at parents or siblings. One child development book (Gesell) said this age gets along with everyone in the family except those between ages 5 and 10. The mother of one child said to him "I'm sorry, dear, that's all we have." Numerous interviews over several years showed that this age gets along best with other 11 ½ and 12 ½ year olds. The problem is they ARE growing up. Sometimes growing between four and six inches a year. Listening to elevens and twelves talking to each other, one hears "I don't want to grow up"—"I want to grow up" and one can hear how ambivalent and torn they are.

These "tweens" feel the chaos of TMI and the codes for "how to be a teenager" all around them. Furthermore they are tired and hungry all the time and "everyone expects too much." Some try a more grown up approach to clothes or other activities in their "survey" and "foraging loops". They may learn from friends or cousins. They may grow three or four inches the same year. Finally the child settles into some order as he or she enters high school at age 14.

Models of Sensemaking

Using three or four theorists in complexity leadership and sensemaking, one can look at models for the "Information Space" for sorting through massive large amounts of data, to coming up with a process that is helpful to reach new knowledge and approaches or "making sense". Peter Petrolli and Stuart Card (1999) laid out the following model which includes new information and processes:

See Sensemaking Model Figure 1.1

These two men, Petrolli and Card, were involved in intelligence work in California, with masses of data (TMI) coming in from many technological sources. There was a need to sort it, reduce the volume as they saw patterns, and look for the story that this data might present. Their model is based on the formula of going from Information; to Schema; to Insights; to Results (or even product). The concept of visualizing information as an aid to thinking is as old as map making and navigational charts (Card, MacKinlay & Schneiderman, 1999). With today's technology it is easier to use "vision as an aid to thinking" especially about complex issues.

In the *Foraging Loop* following chaos and TMI from external data sources, one seeks information, reviews it and takes it in, filters it and extracts information from it, then moves to a "shoebox" step of sorting: tossing out negative evidence and reducing the volume of information. The evidence grows but along selected paths. Then comes problem structuring based on evidence, looking for support or to disconfirm the alternatives; then looking to decision making and choosing a prediction of a course of action from a set of alternatives. The circles in Figure 1.1 represent process flows while the boxes represent data stores. As the knowledge cycle evolves, problems get solved and become undiffused. They even become more concrete and then codified. These results can then become broader and applied to more diffused applications and eventual absorption.

Life Stages and TMI (Too Much Information)

For a child it might be "learn from Suzy" or "try clothes like Katie wears". One starts to make sense of things by holding a larger view or overview that can even be thought of or represented in a schematic way. In the *Sensemaking Loop* the individual "builds a case" starting with two or three hypotheses by adding additional evidence (at age 11 a girl might say "I can look grown up by adding a scarf—I hate jewelry and lose it".) Telling the story begins as one has a more plausible way to present to one's "individual audience" such as parents, workplace colleague's or even one's children. Younger and older people can reject and stretch stereotypes and codes for how to be older children or older adults.

If one looks at these steps in the model as applied to two and three year olds, they become clearer. Two to three year olds still can't talk too well, so they have trouble explaining their ambivalence and frustration. Some are willing to try new things. Some see a friend their age (or even younger) who is toilet trained or who has given up "baby talk". The child can then hypothesize new ways to act, but will swing back and forth. Accidents do happen. Finally they settle into a "mostly trained and mostly acting older mode and become more like a pre-schooler than a toddler—and by now they can talk better. The child is entering a "re-codification" for the new age they've become in this Sensemaking loop. Some children with these behaviors become very secure and are very popular in middle school, but were slow to survey and try out being older before they understood it well enough to "see" it for themselves. Some children just have a longer "foraging loop".

Some life stages have 'codes,' rules or conventions attached to them, which are sometimes exacerbated by the culture of the family or the region around them. Making sense of one's world can run into the presence of barriers that may represent: 1) a conscious attempt to limit diffusion and differentiation; 2) poor communication strategies; and especially 3) a lack of shared context. The groups or individuals may not have seen or experienced what one has seen and experienced. This can especially be seen with those in age groups under 25 or 30; and in fairly rigid enterprises, agencies and cultures.

Groups or people with strongly developed norms concerning how things are done can present some of these barriers. When one conflicts with their well-developed 'common-sense' world view, that one may get discouraged or penalized. For example: "Don't bring that new boyfriend home." Or "don't make waves" in the company. This group may also be used to responding rapidly to well-codified and unambiguous signals. (Such as in the comment "All the ladies [we] all disapproved when Mary's daughter ran off with the postman," etc.) The speaker may respond too fast to allow internalization for the hearers for absorption to occur—that this is a different story being presented than that of Mary's daughter.

However, information may enter from *outside* sources when one tells the hearers stories about friends who did things differently or got engaged to different people. This shows adaptations of girls doing new kinds of things and dating new kinds of people, e.g. scales this coding to a more abstract, broader and diffused perspective. Brainstorming new friends or new trips or other new activities can give local gossip and conversation a new slant for mid-twenties in a similar time warp situation.

According to Boisot (1998) knowledge can be fed in to the process but that doesn't mean it ever will be fully objectively received even by enhancing the understanding of intelligent people. Building the link between codification and complexity can be very complicated and takes time for one to see the new information being received or understood. Again ask: Is the message received in the same way as the message was sent? Is the message received and understood? Is the message acted upon as it was intended? It's important to remember that people don't talk much when they are changing attitudes. These stages that are far-from-equilibrium structures and are called "dissipative" by the literature. This is not a comfortable state to be in. However firms and individuals have to learn to be comfortable in all phases of the Information Space:

- Diffusion;
- Abstraction, and
- Absorption

These then lead to hypotheses, alternatives, and a new codification. Boisot (p. 79) continues that the willingness to try out new codes involves: repetition of new codes; trial and error; and feeling like one is going backward rather than increasing in mastery. Spending time helps learners to increase internalization.

Sometimes spotting new patterns in "generally available information" (for young adults: 'what other *new* things do their parents like?') The "Foresight Diamond" Figure 1.2 shows more ways and approaches for presenting new information. As an 'order' appears the new behaviors or innovations seem less rare.

Figure 1.2 "Foresight Diamond"

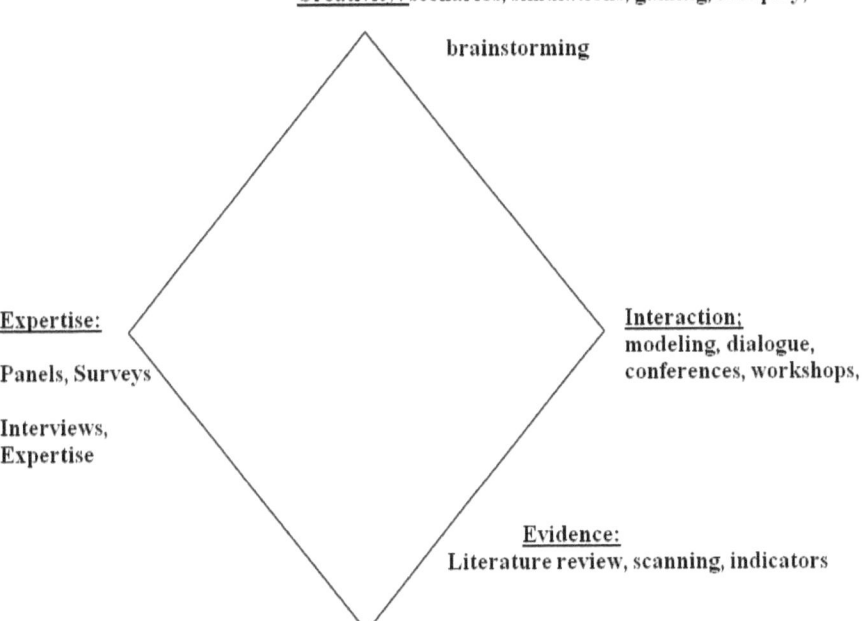

Creativity: scenarios, simulations, gaming, role play, brainstorming

Expertise:

Panels, Surveys

Interviews, Expertise

Interaction;
modeling, dialogue,
conferences, workshops,

Evidence:
Literature review, scanning, indicators

Global Workforce of Tomorrow and Sensemaking

The increasingly diverse and distributed global workforce is changing the way the workforce, including engineers, view education and interact with providers. Today's employers and all engineers and technical individuals need to commit to lifelong learning to succeed in a changing global economy and in work environments that are becoming more virtual and cross-cultural. New generation learners present additional challenges to the way education needs to be delivered. How can universities, industry, public sector groups, and continuing engineering education organizations work together to meet the challenges such as:

1) Knowledge needs in a fast-paced environment
2) Working and learning across boundaries of time and culture
3) Implications of generational shifts in the work force

Innovation means that it is anything but business as usual. The landscape of continuing education is rapidly being transformed by innovations in teaching and learning technology, plus changing student expectations and demands, and novel educational models. Massively Open Online Courses (MOOCs), flipped classrooms, and blended/hybrid learning models are changing the traditional classroom experience.

Processes of dialogue such as listening, respecting, suspending judgment, and voicing provide the 'learning together' environments for essential sensemaking to take place. Once sense is made of complex environments, individuals need to take this newly found knowledge and think about their strategies going forward to give them a new posture in relation to their current environment, culture and existing norms. As one person said "After thinking out of the box, I need to get back into the box to make it work."

The model presented in Figure 1.1 provides an organization for identifying new inputs, technologies and sources of information for the production of new ideas. In intelligence analysis it is seen as a form of sensemaking and an expert skill (Petrolli and Card, 1999). The 'intel' community may see this process modified for changing threats and data characteristics, but for the rest of us a new and useful path for processing an ever-changing world, one's life stages and those of children is available.

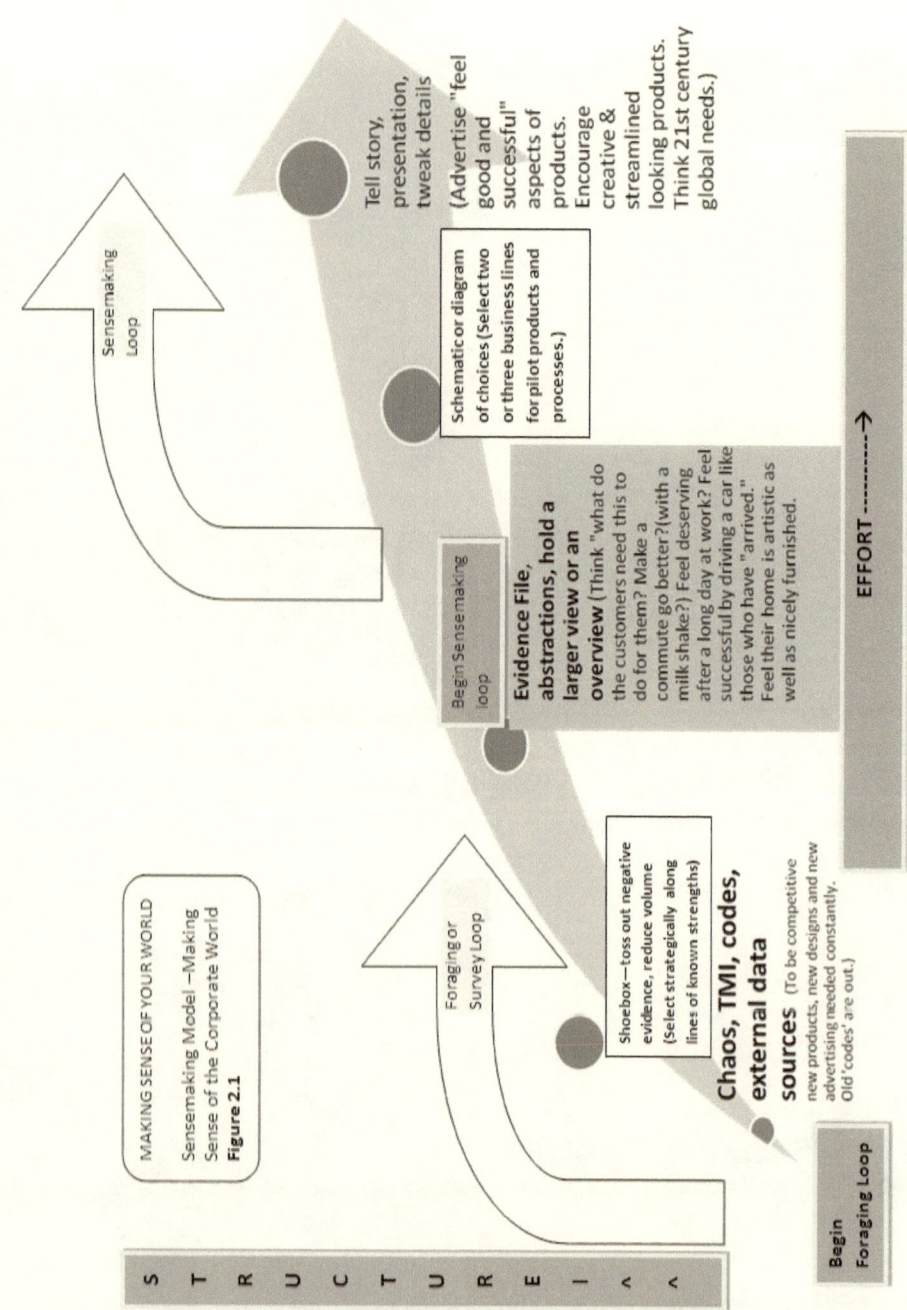

MAKING SENSE OF YOUR WORLD

Sensemaking Model —Making
Sense of the Corporate World
Figure 2.1

Sensemaking
Loop

Begin Sensemaking
loop

Foraging or
Survey Loop

Begin
Foraging Loop

Tell story,
presentation,
tweak details

(Advertise "feel
good and
successful"
aspects of
products.
Encourage
creative &
streamlined
looking products.
Think 21st century
global needs.)

Schematic or diagram
of choices (Select two
or three business lines
for pilot products and
processes.)

**Evidence File,
abstractions, hold a
larger view or an
overview** (Think "what do
the customers need this to
do for them? Make a
commute go better? (with a
milk shake?) Feel deserving
after a long day at work? Feel
successful by driving a car like
those who have "arrived."
Feel their home is artistic as
well as nicely furnished.

**Chaos, TMI, codes,
external data
sources** (To be competitive
new products, new designs and new
advertising needed constantly.
Old 'codes' are out.)

Shoebox—toss out negative
evidence, reduce volume
(Select strategically along
lines of known strengths)

EFFORT - - - - - - →

STRUCTURE IV V

16

Chapter 2

TMI and Chaos
in the Corporate World

Sensemaking started with large corporations that had masses of data coming in on computers and from many channels. Too much information (TMI) has taken over many aspects of corporate life and it also shows up in many stages of life especially for individuals, and especially during any period of life that is in transition. It became clearer that these steps or processes in Sensemaking could be applied to any life stage. (See Part II: Making Sense of Your Life).

It has been found that there is a positive correlation between an organization's ability to make sense of its environment and organizational performance. Improvements in an organization or in an individual's ability to make sense of significant information as it exists currently, or as interpreted to exist in the future, offers opportunities for action that can provide advantage.

A well-constructed sensemaking model was developed by Peter Pirolli and Stuart Card, two intelligence analysts, based on the formula: Information to Outline (or Schema) to Insight to Result (or Product). Their basic chart of Sensemaking presents an understanding of the sensemaking loop as applied to intelligence analysis which includes both data and process flows. This overall depiction is constructed in two major loops: 1) a foraging loop and 2) a sensemaking loop which are helpful in many topic areas.

The Foraging Loop

The model in Figure 2.1 shows an adapted Sensemaking Model building on these basics. The foraging loop seeks information, searching and filtering it, and reading and extracting information. The sensemaking loop then develops a mental model that conceptualizes this information from an outline or schematic that best fits the evidence. Thus focusing on problem structuring—that is the generation, exploration, and management of hypotheses, with reasoning based on evidence—marshalling evidence to support or disconfirm the hypothesis, and decision making—choosing alternatives follows. Then a prediction of a course of action from the set of alternatives comes next. Within this process, cognition is biased towards interpretation of information into existing schemas and expectations and which are subjected to well-documented rules, codes and biases. The circles in the flow chart represent process flows while the boxes indicate data stores (such as 'Too Much Information that can be overwhelming' which resides in the shoebox step). This depiction provides a highly integrated, yet evolutionary methodology for showing the ongoing sensemaking process. In the chart one can see that as effort is put in more structure develops, and becomes clearer. This is true even for ages and stages of human development for children and young adults as in Part II.

Processes of dialogue such as listening, respecting, suspending judgment, and talking together provide the 'learning together' environments for essential strategic sensemaking to take place. Once sense is made of complex environments, organizations and individuals need to learn and understand this newly found knowledge and think about their strategies going forward to give them a new and/or competitive posture. This strategic assimilation, evaluation and planning process is dynamic and ongoing, and is regulated by the front-end sensemaking processes. Strategic knowledge is then captured, shared and transferred to enable critical strategic decisions to be made. In corporations these decisions can support capital investments, change and transformation, and new business models. They can impact on human resource policies and strategies, and on capital improvements. This Strategic Process is ongoing and continuous, and provides an interface with a highly complex and dynamic environment. It can act as a catalyst for organizational plans and strategies.

The role of the Chief Executive Officer (CEO) can best be understood as both sensemaker and sensegiver. In this role the CEO develops a sense of the organization's internal and external environment. He or she defines the revised conception of the organization, develops new interpretations and creates the abstract vision of the changed organization. Then the CEO communicates the new constructs through sensegiving processes. Complex development projects require flexible organizational networks and open communication to generate sufficient levels of sensemaking for innovation, according to Moss (2001). Moss underscores that the interwoven relationship between sensemaking, complexity and knowledge is a relationship well suited to adaptive systems, which respond to their increasingly complex environments.

Reduce the Volume, Toss Out Negative Evidence, the Shoe Box step

In one example of corporate sensemaking, one can look at General Motors (GM) in 2012. In making sense of a large corporation, Randy Mott, new 2012 CIO and Vice-President of GM, sees himself as joining a "$150 billion startup" according to a July 2012 interview in *Information Week*. General Motors was like being "fresh from an IPO" after the U.S. Treasury bailed it out according to Mott. Treasury still owned 26% of the corporation at that time in 2012. He was pleased to be at GM as very few global corporations have an "appetite for change," he said. With his role came hard choices and strategic sensemaking.

He noted that the customer data was in a number of different silos with warranty information in one place, VIN (vehicle identification numbers) and parts numbers in another, and social media analyses in still another silo. Newer technology made bringing all this IT into one data architecture as a way to reduce the volume of all this information (TMI) and integrate it. This integration served as one of the alternatives for selection for a new presentation of the "stories" of the corporation. This was to integrate the data and make it more accessible. Another selected alternative was to re-organize the IT every year based on business goals, rather than on a rigid information technology (IT) organization chart. A third alternative might be to coordinate advertising with articles running in the press, using the newly accessible customer data.

Take a Larger View or Overview

Customer data has always been important but in 1960 Ernest Dichter, a Viennese psychologist, published a book named *"The Strategy of Desire."* As a trained psychoanalyst, Dichter saw motivation as being two-thirds unseen, much like an iceberg, and even unknown to the consumer. Psychological differences and brand images came into their own as new advertising influences. Dichter became famous for helping large corporations selling soap or cars (including GM) position their products as desirable for many reasons, not just as useful or practical (Dec. 2011, *The Economist*, pp. 119-123).

For instance, soap had a "personality" to "give you a fresh start" or with Ivory soap "to wash your troubles away." Dichter felt that opportunities for seeking pleasure and fulfillment in everyday purchases was a value to be touted. In booming late twentieth century America, this worked really well. Dichter saw that brands in this new world had become a "substitute for nobility and the family tree." This theme in advertising can be seen on a global scale today.

With the advent of computers rapidly improving IT research information, and criticism about "The Affluent American" and from Betty Friedan on gender issues, some of this manipulation by advertisers was dampened. The onslaught of "too much information" (TMI) began and has been multiplied today by the advertising industry coming full circle back to the emotion and unconscious subliminal approaches now which are back in style. A new framework of assumptions has been built, and new ways to tell stories about purchasing choices has been developed. It is known, for instance, that testimonials are effective with certain market segments. The stories of what motivates people according to Dichter are still viewed as some of the best approaches around.

Select Two or Three Alternatives

Reducing the volume of data might mean looking at two or three models of the new approach to new products. Some of the following examples can yield insights. Corporations would focus on building the management and innovation capacity of designers, engineers, and business people who wish to be a creative force, working in the world of business. Some higher education programs assist students to gain a competitive advantage as leaders through a variety of means even with a particular focus on design thinking.

In her 2008 *New York Times* article on the rise of right brain thinkers in the business world, Janet Rae-Dupree quotes Albert Einstein who said, "Imagination is more important than knowledge." She then explains how the computational skills that our economy once valued are now easily outsourced and that computers can handle . . . "many of the sequential skills of the brain's left hemisphere." Her analysis is in line with that of Daniel Pink, the author of *A Whole New Mind: Why Right Brainers will Rule the Future* (2006), who also argues that ". . . it's time for our imaginative right brain to take center stage." This idea is not new but has gained greater attention in the last decade.

As the knowledge cycle evolves, problems get solved and become undiffused, codified and more concrete. Further evolution provides an abstraction of knowledge so that it can be applied and diffused to broader applications for eventual absorption and impact on society. This cycle can be applied to understanding strategic learning and interfaces with the environment for new knowledge creation and for competitive value. From lower to higher the sensemaking plane interfaces with the environment where sensemaking occurs.

Figure 2.1A

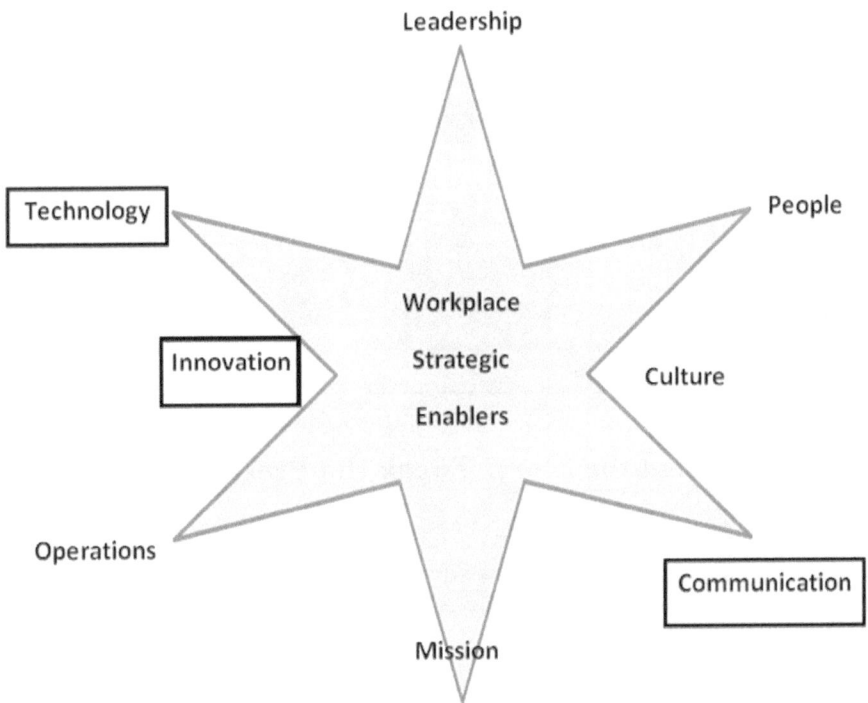

In selecting two or three alternatives one might select only two or three of the Workplace Strategic Enablers shown in Figure 2.1a. If an organization is analyzing its present and planning for the future, selecting two or three enablers such as Innovation, Communication and Technology might be logical places to start. One can then focus small groups on these three to see what the groups develop for further consideration as Action Plans. This diagram (Figure 2.1a) shows the eight categories of Workplace Strategic Enablers. These Enablers can be taken up, a few at a time. They are under development for a future book by this writer and are among the usual areas that leaders choose for future planning.

Figure 2.2 Knowledge Cycle (adapted from Boisot, 1998)

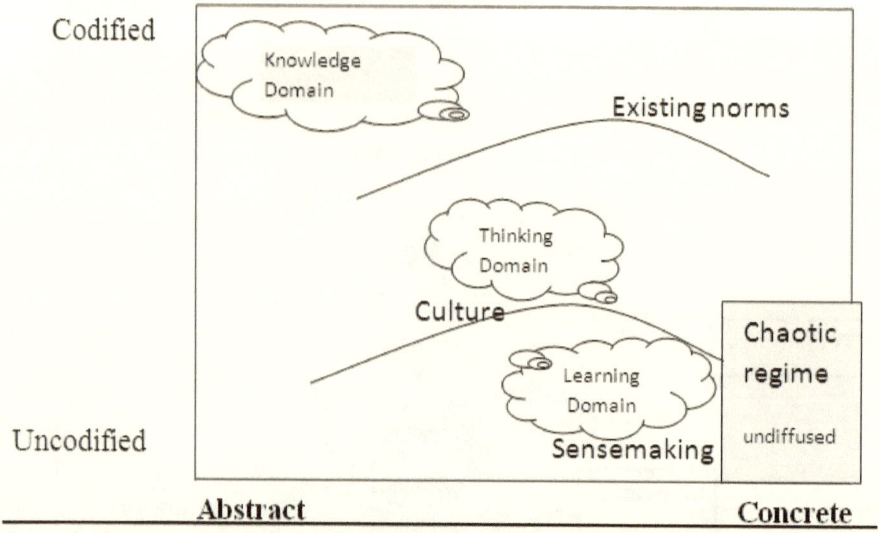

Present the Story, Tweak the Presentation

The logical next step from given sensemaking activities concerning new products, new approaches and new advertising, is to present this information and new vision to peers, employees and the general public. As the new, innovative ways of doing things become codified somewhat on their own, the feeling of chaos and TMI subsides in that particular arena.

Corporations have been described as distributed knowledge systems and as dynamic webs of sensemaking processes. As these organizations face increasingly complex competitive environments, thinking processes such as sensemaking can be catalysts for adding valuable insights and actions. These environments are expected to continue to increase in complexity over time as the impact of globalization, technology, and other key factors such as political, economic, social, technological and even operational factors evolve and rapidly emerge. The dynamic organizations that are able to keep pace with these changes and offer consistently competitive value propositions, will have a competitive advantage and an increased probability of sustainability. However, the challenges and complexity associated with these environmental changes are extraordinary and require competence in sensemaking processes that are strategic in response. Making sense of these increasingly ambiguous, unclear, unsuspected circumstances, threats, and opportunities provide important insights needed to excel in today's global market economy. Gray and Vander Wal (2012) say that "without organizational and management innovation, business model innovation and adaptation to today's fast-changing world innovation, rarely happens."

The concept of sensemaking is about making sense, a cognitive process that occurs within individuals, teams, groups, organizations and in many kinds of enterprises. The processes that are used to make sense in corporations are thinking, learning, knowledge, strategy development, organizational diagnosis, transformation and change, and communication. Making sense in these and other areas is an important enabler for organizations and almost all of them are also enablers for individuals. Developing new models, theories, tools, and practices offer new and important insights that can contribute to organizational performance. Sensemaking has been described as environmental scanning, interpretation, and associated responses (Thomas, Clark, Gioia, 1993). "Sensemaking is a process in which individuals develop cognitive maps of their environment" (Gioia, Chittipeddi, 1991, p.444). "Sensemaking seeks to establish objective knowledge of subjective processes," said another theorist. Weick (1995) has proposed that "sensemaking is about such things as placement of items into frameworks, comprehending (*handling*) surprise, constructing meaning, interacting in pursuit of mutual understanding, and patterning" (Weick, 1995, p. 6). The difference between interpretation and sensemaking is that "sensemaking is about the ways people generate what they interpret" and is "clearly an activity or a process whereas interpretation can be a process but is just as likely to describe a product." "To engage in sensemaking is to construct, filter, frame, create" and take action to transform the subjective into the objective (Weick, 1995).

Sensemaking and strategic activities are both retrospective in nature as well as future-focused. Developing a shared meaning and understanding as the result of conversation, dialogue and interaction is an important part of the sensemaking process. These social sensemaking processes play an essential role in understanding, assimilating and taking action on strategically relevant information.

Strategic sensemaking touches on cognitive processes such as: thinking, learning and decision-making. Associated terms relating to sensemaking in organizations include affiliations with learning, thinking, transformation, knowledge, complex adaptive systems, innovation, improvisation and in corporations the management domains. At an organizational level, sensemaking is associated with taking action and action theories. The sensemaking process provides interpretive capability for structuring diffuse, diverse or ambiguous information so that it can be associated with frameworks, with a diagram or schematic and reasoning, to create meaning and insights that support action and decision-making.

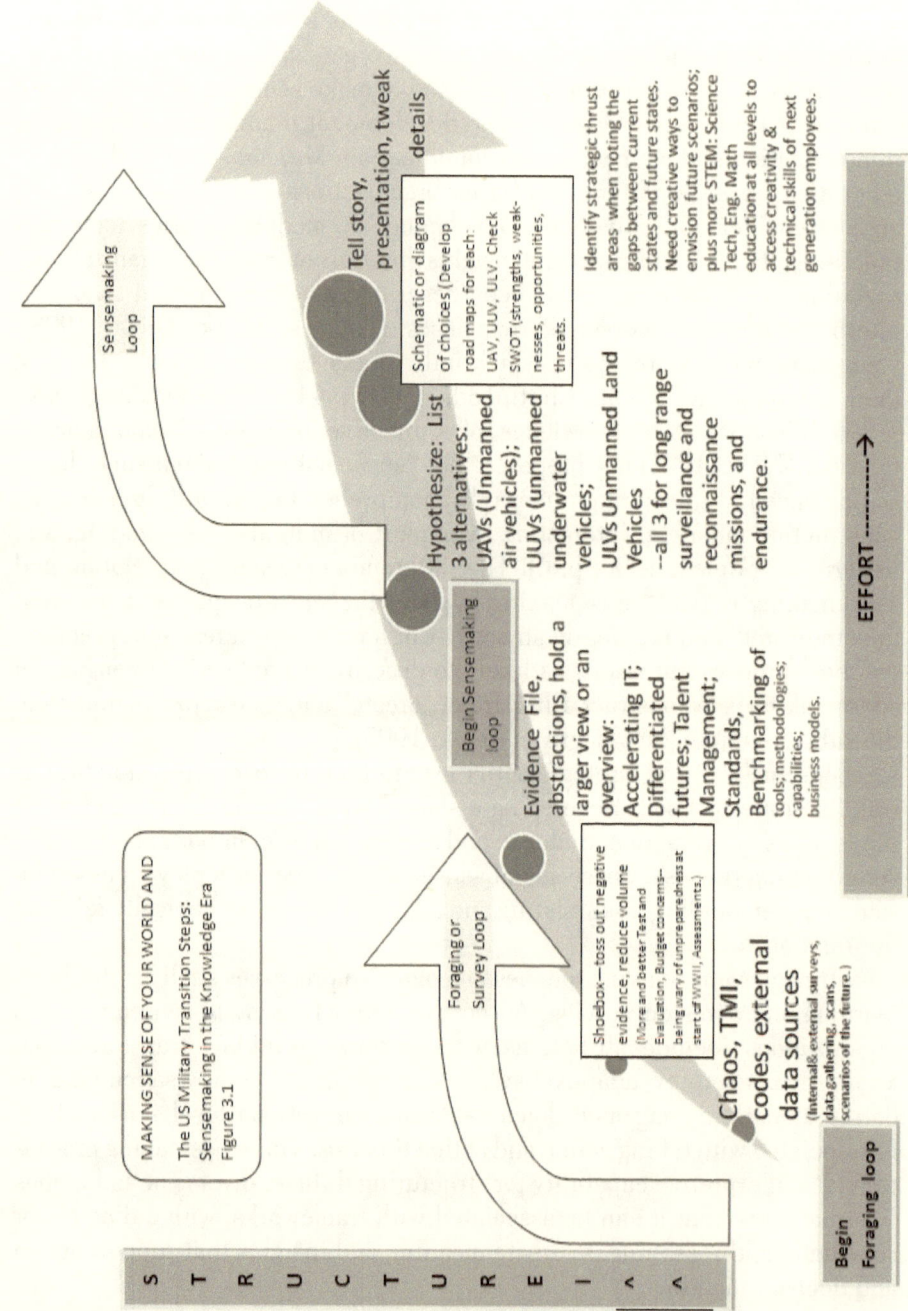

MAKING SENSE OF YOUR WORLD AND

The US Military Transition Steps:
Sensemaking in the Knowledge Era
Figure 3.1

Sensemaking Loop

Foraging or Survey Loop

Tell story, presentation, tweak details

Schematic or diagram of choices (Develop road maps for each: UAV, UUV, ULV. Check SWOT (strengths, weaknesses, opportunities, threats.

Hypothesize: List 3 alternatives: UAVs (Unmanned air vehicles); UUVs (unmanned underwater vehicles; ULVs Unmanned Land Vehicles –all 3 for long range surveillance and reconnaissance missions, and endurance.

Identify strategic thrust areas when noting the gaps between current states and future states. Need creative ways to envision future scenarios; plus more STEM: Science Tech, Eng. Math education at all levels to access creativity & technical skills of next generation employees.

Begin Sensemaking loop

Evidence File, abstractions, hold a larger view or an overview: Accelerating IT; Differentiated futures; Talent Management; Standards, Benchmarking of tools; methodologies; capabilities; business models.

Shoebox—toss out negative evidence, reduce volume (More and better Test and Evaluation. Budget concerns—being wary of unpreparedness at start of WWII, Assessments.)

Chaos, TMI, codes, external data sources (Internal & external surveys, data gathering, scans, scenarios of the future.)

EFFORT ------->

S T R U C T U R E   I N   A A

Begin Foraging loop

24

Chapter 3

The U.S. Military Services: Making Sense in Leadership Shifting from the Industrial Age to the Information Age with Complexity Leadership

Complexity science suggests a different paradigm for leadership from command and control—one that frames leadership as a complex, interactive dynamic from which adaptive outcomes, such as learning, innovation and adaptability emerge. This statement is according to Marion Uhl-Bien (2007) in an article with colleagues from the Leadership Institute. Building the foundations for 'how we think' requires strategic thinking, strategic planning and later strategic operations, and is needed across the U.S. Military according to thought leaders in the services. Strategic ability is about how thought leaders develop an ability to place knowledge in new contexts and understand the domains of future scenarios. This may mean having a "Command Information Center"(CIC) to process all the analytics, as one service has, in which "CICs" are duplicated across their command. "It's all about learning and thinking" said a leader in one service, as Dale Moore, a Navair strategic thought leader, said in a speech on "Strategic Thinking" (2012), to a large group of corporate business leaders.

Systems thinking in an agency or a corporation can help people see an old issue in a new perspective. Even overhead costs can be seen as like the oil in a car engine. One shouldn't reduce it too much or the car won't run well. Strategic thinking is discovering novel and imaginative strategies which can re-write rules and envision potential futures that may be significantly different from today. The differences between strategic and operational thinking needed for developing director and executive competencies in strategic thinking according to Phil Hanford (1996) can be seen in the chart below:

Strategic Thinking	Operational Thinking
Longer Term	Immediate Term
Conceptual	Concrete
Reflective/Learning	Action/Doing
ID of Key Issues/Opportunities	Resolution of Existing Performance Problems
Breaking New Ground	Routine/Ongoing
Effectiveness	Efficiency
Hands-off Approach	Hands-on Approach
"Helicopter" Perspective	'On-the-Ground' Perspective

Information is viewed not as a "thing" or fact but as an energy which can be seen in an organization that is redesigning itself because of 'access' to information, and this includes the U. S. Armed Services. Both the Army and the Marines now have the technology to provide every individual soldier with information about what's happening on the battlefront. This information was formerly known only to the commanders, according to Margaret Wheatley in *Leadership and the New Science* (1999, 2006).

"The Army has discovered that when individuals have such information and know how to interpret it,—because they know 'the commander's intent' and goals, they can make decisions that lead to greater success in battle. The individuals respond quickly and intelligently and assume responsibility for their decisions." (M. Wheatley, 1994).

"A network form of organization, linked together by technology and shared meaning makes the soldier more effective" they found.

Greater openness can be a path to greater order also became clearer, as scientists studied nature and the order and systems that develop in a larger picture and bigger, longer view of a system such as those found in science. The larger picture also shows that even differing from historical traditions is possible in the greater search for effectiveness, and any organization that wants to learn has to look at new information that is at odds with past beliefs and practices. The Army, the service under study by Wheatley, has known that intuition plays a role in commanders' effectiveness even to the point of studying "commander intuition."

Generating Sensemaking into the Future

Strategic sensemaking plays a fundamental role in creating competitive advantage for corporations or for government agencies seeking to perform better in their mission. Keeping America safe now and in the future has always been the purpose of the U.S. military forces and DOD agencies. The sensemaking role is increasingly significant as environments, internally and externally, become more complex and dynamic. Organizational leaders and managers will need to continually make sense of ongoing and long range environments and then to reflect them back into organizational decisions, strategies and plans according to Moore (2012). Sensemaking provides an initial interface with a complex internal and external environment, and can provide an enabling capability to make sense of the required and requisite complexity needed for complexity leadership, and thus provide the fodder for strategic decisions and actions.

Sensemaking plays an essential role in critical situations to make sense of ambiguity, complexity and chaos. Sensemaking remains an integral component in strategic learning as it has roots in transformation and change which can stem from both sensemaking and sensegiving. A number of models exist in the literature, which depict the sensemaking process, its ongoing and interactive nature, and its role as fodder for the strategic processes of learning, thinking, knowledge and decisions as mentioned above.

Processes of dialogue such as listening, respecting, suspending and voicing provide the environment for essential strategic sensemaking to take place and for needed interactions with a wide variety of people and settings. Significant efforts into foresight methodologies provide rich opportunities to accelerate the process of making sense of the complexity and chaos inherent in the future. The Foresight Diamond (adapted here from Popper, 2008) articulates a broad range of evidence based, expertise-based, creativity-based, and interaction-based methods for gaining foresight. More activities for use for this purpose can be found in the literature.

Figure 3.2 Foresight Diamond:
Helps in Making Sense Strategically

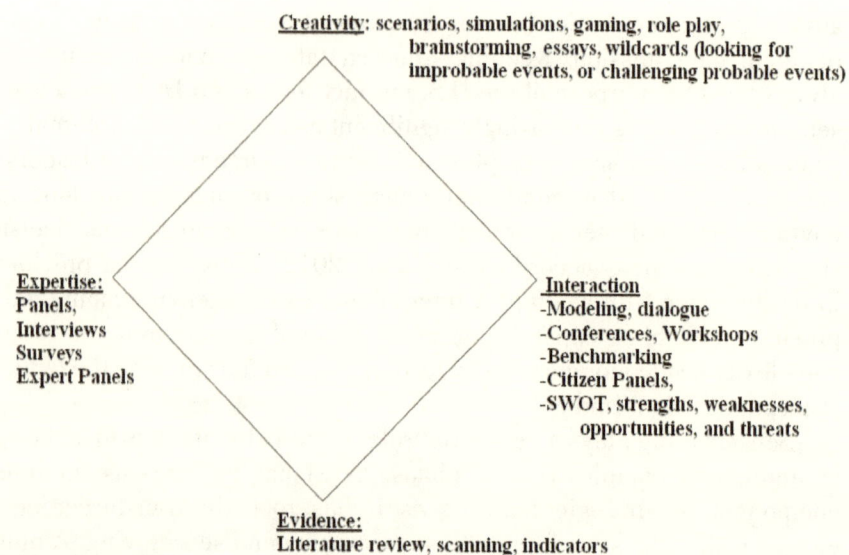

Creativity: scenarios, simulations, gaming, role play,
brainstorming, essays, wildcards (looking for
improbable events, or challenging probable events)

Expertise:
Panels,
Interviews
Surveys
Expert Panels

Interaction
-Modeling, dialogue
-Conferences, Workshops
-Benchmarking
-Citizen Panels,
-SWOT, strengths, weaknesses,
opportunities, and threats

Evidence:
Literature review, scanning, indicators

(Adapted from Popper 2008)

Expertise: *Interaction*

Panels,   - **Modeling, dialogue**

Interviews   - **Conferences, Workshops**

Surveys   - **Benchmarking**

Expert Panels   - **Citizen Panels,**

                                     - **SWOT, strengths, weaknesses,
                                       opportunities, and threats**

Evidence:
Literature review, scanning, indicators

(Adapted from Popper 2008)

Strategic sensemaking is an important component for sustaining and generating concepts to future generations. As new technologies evolve and enable the acceleration of the strategic sensemaking of complexity, those that embrace and explore new domains of knowledge through socializing, piloting ideas, and experimenting will accelerate their learning in areas they need that are strategic. Thus they position themselves for a high probability of this learning being sustained over the long term. A more detailed version of the Foresight diamond might look like this:

Figure 3.3 Detailed Foresight Diamond

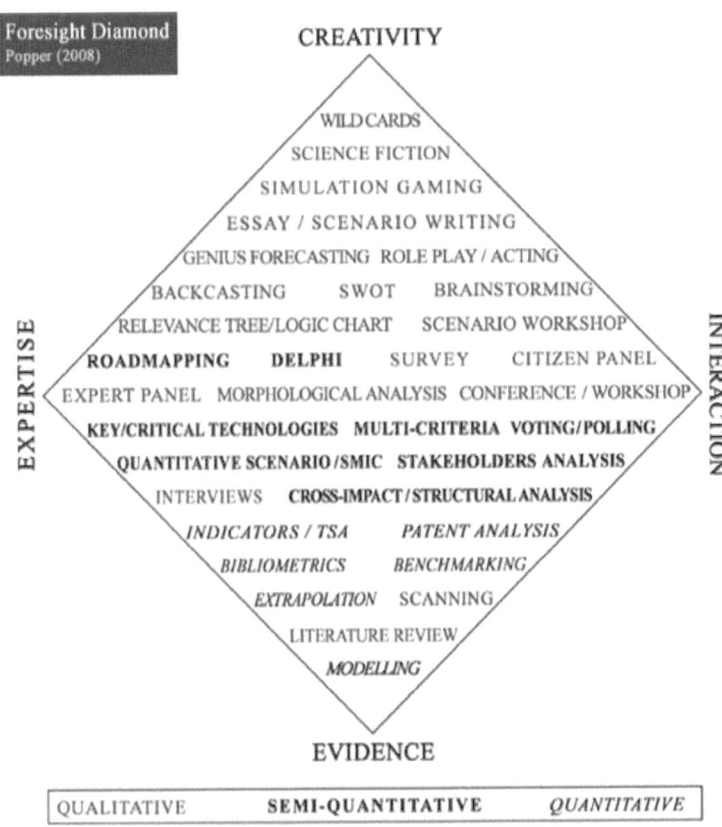

Strategic thinking as 'seeing' might look like Figure 3.4 as one 'thinks through' a specific project (adapted from Mintzberg, 1994). Thinking of an enterprise as an ecosystem with a strategic value stream that is highly complex, interfacing with many other of the 50 or so agencies in the Department of Defense (DOD), also gives new insights.

Figure 3.4 Thinking Through and 'Seeing'

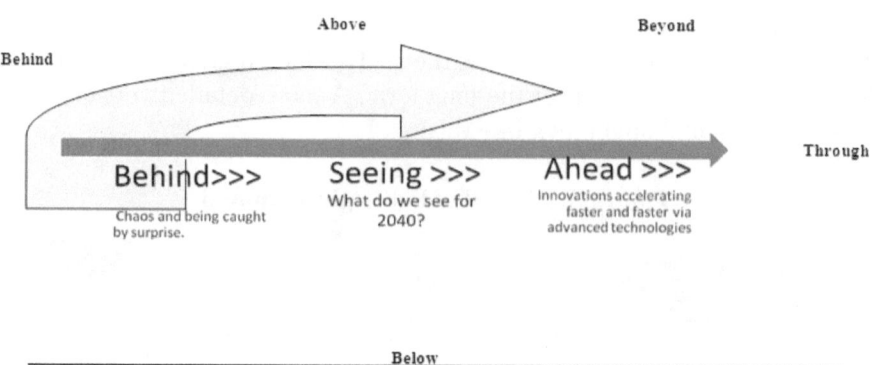

Strategic thinking as 'seeing' can deliver insights, best practices and innovations in strategy and execution. Thinking about the extreme future and thinking like a futurist further enables this process.

Innovations are accelerating faster and faster via advanced technologies with the only limits being: How well are we aware of what's happening? What will be happening in 2040?

How we can use it? and

How can we lead to move forward? The need for strategic sensemaking only grows. This can include:

- Strategic learning and new capabilities
- Re-generative and sustainability initiatives
- Technological limits to advancement, as the technology paradigm becomes ever more dominant. For example one theorist says that desktop computers will be 64,000 times more powerful in 2032 than they were in 2012.

A transformational paradigm shift is coming in as the old incremental theories of leadership are being overtaken by events according to DISA (Defense Information Systems Agency). This is more appropriate for times that are:

- volatile,
- uncertain,
- complex, and
- ambiguous.

In the Sensemaking model for this chapter *Too much information* (TMI) for the U.S. Military includes scans bringing in massive amounts of data from all over the world. These may cover the main issues around particular sectors. Making sense of this input is a gargantuan task but necessary.

In the *'shoebox'* step reducing the volume and tossing out negative evidence with testing and evaluation for all new products under consideration becomes vital across all the services. A tank that has its satellite dish blown off in a high wind in the middle-eastern desert should have been tested more thoroughly. The contractor saying "it never did that in the lab" doesn't solve this expensive problem.

In the *evidence file*—a larger abstraction shows that the acceleration of information technology requires a long view of many possible differentiated scenarios in the future. Talent management to develop these skills is needed, as well as standards and benchmarking applied to tools, methodologies, capabilities and new business models.

In complexity theory and complexity leadership one can get the butterfly effect: A small change now can lead to a big change later just as a caterpillar turns into a butterfly, but are all a part of the same system. There is a call for DOD and the Navy and other services to maximize the strengths they have to balance the threats that may be in the future. The people-side of this concern includes awareness of how information and communication is handled. Future system relevance versus future threats will require future infrastructure relevance and capabilities. Daniel Pink, in his book *Drive* (2009) states that people are intrinsically motivated to work on something they value and believe in. Keeping the nation safe is a highly held value. Pink goes on to say that intrinsic motivation has an inestimable return on investment (ROI). He also says that meaningful achievement means lifting one's sights and pushing the horizon. "Greatness is incompatible with nearsightedness" (p. 57). *Telling the story* and enunciating the vision will be a continuing effort.

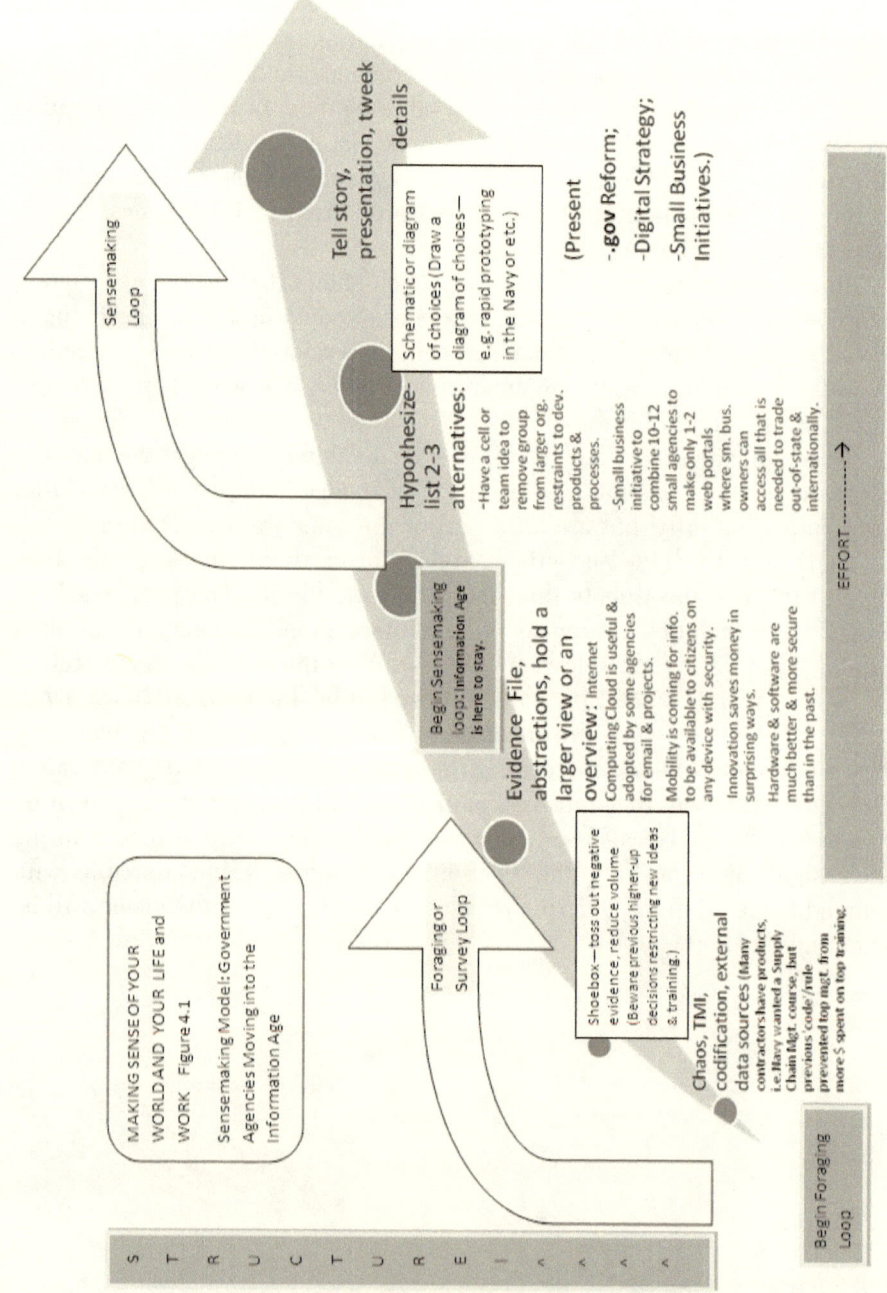

MAKING SENSE OF YOUR WORLD AND YOUR LIFE and WORK   Figure 4.1

Sensemaking Model: Government Agencies Moving into the Information Age

Sensemaking Loop

Foraging or Survey Loop

Begin Foraging Loop

STRUCTURE ↑↑↑

Tell story, presentation, tweek details

Schematic or diagram of choices (Draw a diagram of choices— e.g: rapid prototyping in the Navy or etc.)

(Present
-**gov Reform**;
-**Digital Strategy**;
-Small Business Initiatives.)

Hypothesize- list 2-3 alternatives:

-Have a cell or team idea to remove group from larger org. restraints to dev. products & processes.

-Small business initiative to combine 10-12 small agencies to make only 1-2 web portals where sm. bus. owners can access all that is needed to trade out-of-state & internationally.

EFFORT --------→

Begin Sensemaking loop: Information Age is here to stay.

Evidence File, abstractions, hold a larger view or an overview: Internet Computing Cloud is useful & adopted by some agencies for email & projects.

Mobility is coming for info. to be available to citizens on any device with security.

Innovation saves money in surprising ways.

Hardware & software are much better & more secure than in the past.

Shoebox—toss out negative evidence, reduce volume (Beware previous higher-up decisions restricting new ideas & training.)

Chaos, TMI, codification, external data sources (Many contractors have products, i.e. Navy wanted a Supply Chain Mgt. course, but previous 'code'/rule prevented top mgt. from more $ spent on top training.

32

Chapter 4

Make Sense in Government Agencies: IT with Too Much Information and Chaos

Trends in Information Technology (IT) have been multiplying fast and in the corporate world new theories are becoming available for making sense of the masses of information and innovation now available. A combination of two theories or models (Boiset 1999, Petrolli and Card 1999) make a good framework that developed for this book with an early title of "From CHAOS to Making Sense in Your World: Sensemaking in Your Life". This framework builds on taking an issue from a Chaos situation to a Thinking Domain to a Knowledge Domain. The Knowledge Domain can have filters and codes interfering, often based on a culture. The framework used here for Sensemaking has five steps in it as has been shown for corporations.

In this book, the last seven chapters are on stages in human development in which 'too much information' is a problem such as: Mid-20's; Ages 13-15 Years; Dealing with Serious Illness; and Later Life, and others. The early three chapters of the book are on Sensemaking in the Corporate World, Sensemaking in the U.S. Department of Defense; and Sensemaking in the other 57 or so U.S. Federal agencies and departments which is in material presented and taken from years of membership in the Federal Association for Information Resource Management (AFFIRM).

The U.S. Federal government is spending $80-$100 billion dollars a year on information technology (IT). In the last twenty years the process of moving aspects of various large government agencies into consolidating basic IT services and making information available and accessible to citizens in many ways, is an example of moving from the *chaos* of too much information into a *foraging or surveying loop* and on to selected alternatives for ways to reach for the thinking and knowledge domains. Culture, Codes and Filters can slow this down. For example in the early days the Chief Information Officer (CIO) of the Environmental Protection Agency (EPA) and the CIO of the Department of Education were heard agreeing that a good "Internet Policy" was to allow employees to use the Internet only on their lunch hours.

Poor quality technology and numerous proprietary IT systems contributed to a problem yielding feelings of chaos among employees and too much information (TMI) especially from vendors. In the late 1990's one agency had eight separate telephone systems that crashed almost daily according to their CIO. Another agency, the Veterans Administration, had one old computer on every floor. They said "some employees still prefer manual typewriters." In 2013 one agency had 23 virtual networks.

Slowly from all external data sources an effort to *reduce the volume of data and toss out negative evidence* emerged in different agencies for different systems. The Department of Defense (DOD) decided to focus on "non-secure" (meaning non-national security) areas for IT savings, according to Dr. Andrew Usher, Defense Analyst and Professor of Policy Analysis for George Washington University, such as:

Commissaries
Post and Base Exchanges
Depots
Medical Centers
Transportation, and
Fiscal and paycheck Centers.

While these areas each then went through the Sensemaking Steps of *foraging for possibilities* and models, then selecting alternatives, the Defense Finance and Accounting Services Agency (DFAS) emerged. The more than 100 Defense Finance Data Centers were consolidated to fewer than 17 under DFAS.

Enormous financial benefits began to be realized with consolidation. Other agencies began "outsourcing" excess IT capacity to sister agencies. For example the Department of Agriculture (USDA) was able to handle the Human Resources IT needs for another large agency, thus consolidating It resources, IT support, and IT purchases in a "fee for service" shared services arrangement.

In "telling the story" DOD had to overcome some barriers and "tweak the presentation" to address four military services learning to work together and fear of the "purple suit Pentagon." The paychecks continued to be on-time and handled just as well as ever by DFAS.

Further alternatives pending across federal government agencies include more:

Data Center Consolidation;
Shared Services;
Mobility;
Bring Your Own Device (BYOD);
Cloud Computing; and
Secure Framework(s).

Each of these areas could also have their own Sensemaking Chart to sort through too much information, model after best practices, select alternatives and present their story to those affected by the plan, some of whom had input into its development. Another noteworthy consolidation effort which yields new kinds of benefits, is the grouping of 17 intelligence agencies under the National Director of Intelligence Agency (NDIA). The FBI, CIA, all the Service Intelligences agencies such as the Naval Intelligence Service, DIA and various Army and Air Force Agencies are included in this wide-ranging information sharing resource.

Federal government agencies have been moving into the Knowledge Era with initiatives like the "Federal Digital Strategy" for quite some time. As seen in the "steps to Sensemaking Model" diagram, first there was "too much information (TMI)", and chaos from external data sources such as many contractors with proprietary products. Then came a "shoebox" stage of reducing volume and tossing out negative evidence. This was helped by the advent of cloud computing and data center consolidation. As cloud computing and data center consolidation have become useful and adopted by some agencies, so is "mobility" with showing a shoebox effect of reducing volume. The goal was for mobility to make "information available to citizens on any device on any platform," and also within an agency depending on security needs. The question of "apps" (applications) was not to be the defining issue.

It was acknowledged that the Federal Digital Strategy(2012) was becoming less about devices and apps and more about giving agencies a roadmap to improve functions and interactions with citizens and businesses. The Office of Management and Budget (OMB) was expected to release the digital services strategy in summer 2012. The new focus of the strategy was based on the Administration's desire to focus more broadly on *how* and *when* data is delivered, and not about the devices. The digital strategy includes mobile and the **.gov** reform effort.

The task force report on **.gov** reform, released in December, 2011, found that 19 percent of all sites were inactive, and agencies planned now to terminate or merge 442 sites in that coming year. The **.gov** reform effort then and now is less about reducing the number of domains and web sites and more about ensuring that agency web sites are able to provide easy access to data from anywhere at any time and now from any device. Another goal was to ensure that websites are not too clogged with over 1,000 links on the homepage as was the homepage of the Federal Communications Commission (FCC).

Based upon input from agencies and industry experts on OMB's draft mobile strategy concept released in 2011, going digital means making sure data is built right from the beginning, that it's open and that content is created that can be delivered through multiple channels. This was and is not about technology but about how the government can deliver better on the mission agenda of the specific agency.

A cornerstone of the strategy is security and privacy. The digital strategy will really talk about data—how to build the data and provide good content that's delivered anywhere, anytime and in a secure way. Speakers are offering insights on strategic sourcing plans for devices and services, and how agencies can work more closely with industry to improve how data is delivered to citizens.

In the *Evidence File* step in the model it has been found that innovation and sharing services between and among agencies saves money in surprising ways. Hardware and software are now much better and more secure-able than in the past. The Federal Office of Management and Budget (OMB) wanted agencies to know when its time to implement shared services for categories (also called commodities) such as Human Resources (HR). First steps included the government talking to itself and within agencies about possibilities. However by looking for ways to share 'commodity' IT (Information Technologies) in support of IT and in mission IT between agencies and within agencies, some savings could be realized in the $80 billion Federal IT budget in 2012. These shared services are seen as part of IT reform. "Best Practices" can be shared across all the agencies according to Dr. Scott Bernard, Federal Chief Enterprise Architect at OMB. Two agencies, GSA (Government Services Agency) and USDA (US Dept. of Agriculture) have migrated from hundreds of mobile contracts to three, thus saving 10% or more of that cost. Clearly OMB is still in the "data collection" stage they have stated. The Dept. of Interior is already saving $100 million a year with some consolidation and shared services he reported. So thus we see that Sensemaking in the (IT) information technology world can have many benefits in aspects affecting much of an enterprise including costs.

Making Sense
of Life Stages and TMI

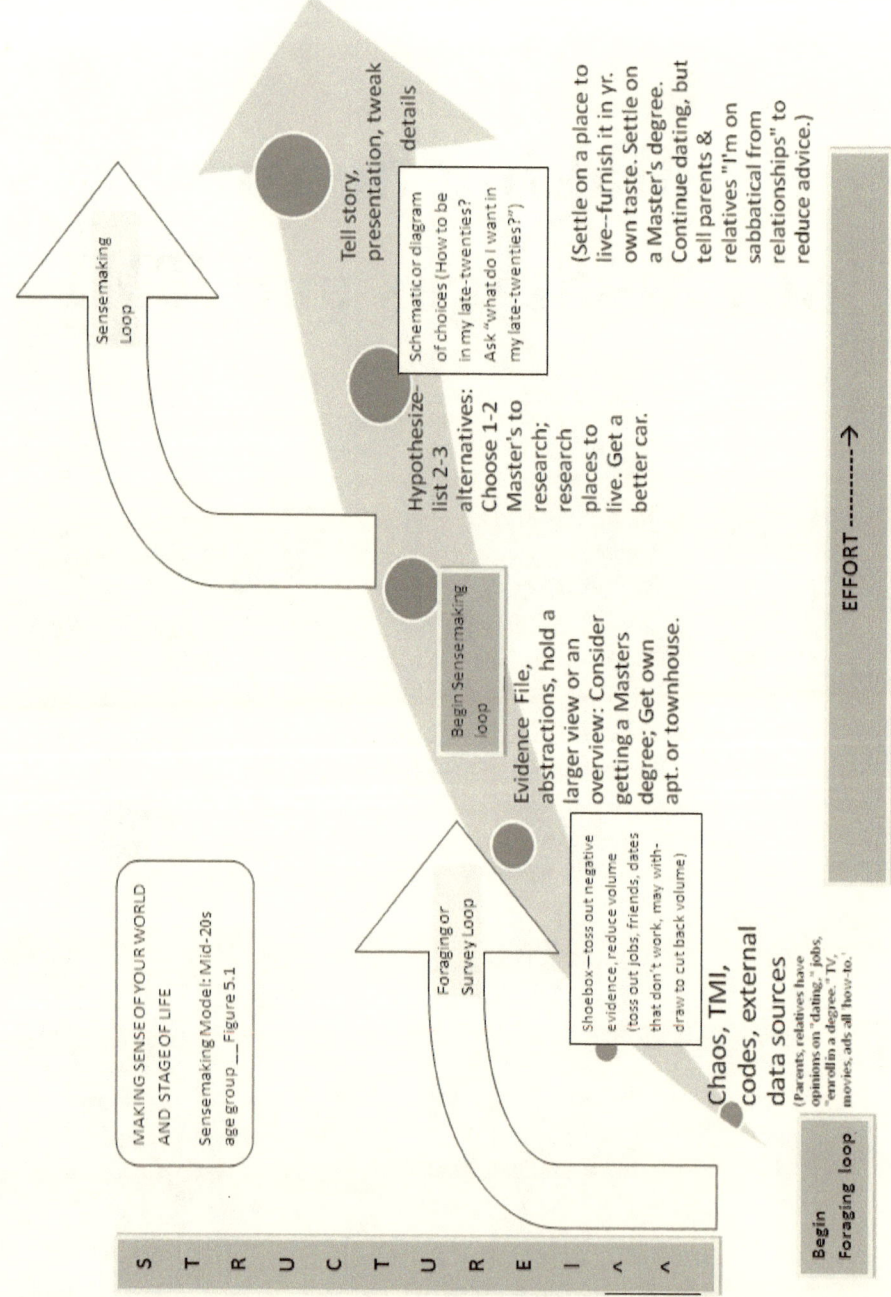

MAKING SENSE OF YOUR WORLD AND STAGE OF LIFE

Sensemaking Model: Mid-20s age group __ Figure 5.1

Sensemaking Loop

Foraging or Survey Loop

Begin Sensemaking loop

Begin Foraging loop

Tell story, presentation, tweak details

Schematic or diagram of choices (How to be in my late-twenties? Ask "what do I want in my late-twenties?")

(Settle on a place to live—furnish it in yr. own taste. Settle on a Master's degree. Continue dating, but tell parents & relatives "I'm on sabbatical from relationships" to reduce advice.)

Hypothesize-list 2-3 alternatives: Choose 1-2 Master's to research; research places to live. Get a better car.

Evidence File, abstractions, hold a larger view or an overview: Consider getting a Masters degree; Get own apt. or townhouse.

Shoebox—toss out negative evidence, reduce volume (toss out jobs, friends, dates that don't work, may withdraw to cut back volume)

Chaos, TMI, codes, external data sources (Parents, relatives have opinions on "dating," jobs, "enroll in a degree," TV, movies, ads all how-to.)

STRUCTURE

EFFORT ------→

Chapter 5

Making Sense of
Too Much Information (TMI)
in the Mid-Twenties

"Why does everyone give me so much advice?" might well be the question of many in their middle-twenty years. Using the sensemaking model and gathering the information needed for steps in it, will help one to see situations in a new light and possibly reveal hidden problems that can be solved. For the last 20 to 30 years, certainly in the Information Age, this age group has been a hard period for those newly finished attending college. Life is no longer clear, with a set goal like getting into (or out of) college. "I feel like I'm in eighth grade again; worrying about what comes next" was the comment of several. The feelings of 'chaos' in the mid-twenties are also exacerbated by Too Much Information (TMI) from advertising, movies, TV, social networking plus parents and relatives. Much information about what make-up to buy, what body-image to pursue, what car to buy and more, is pushed at this age group by the almost $100 billion advertising industry. A good segment of this is also pushed at teens, tweenagers, and preschoolers. Slowly one can start reducing the volume by tossing out negative evidence such as "longer eyelashes do NOT guarantee happiness," and also discarding negative friends, dates, advice and electronic input. Parents and relatives that may be asking "why don't you find a *nice* person to date?" begin to be shut out.

Some life stages have 'codes' attached to them, which are sometimes exaggerated by the culture of the family or the region around them. Making sense of one's world can run into the presence of barriers that may represent: 1) a conscious attempt to limit diffusion and differentiation; 2) poor communication strategies; and 3) especially a lack of shared context. These groups or individuals may not have seen or experienced what this 20-something person has seen or experienced. This can be observed particularly with those in age groups under 25 or 30; or in fairly rigid enterprises, corporations and agencies.

Groups or people with strongly developed norms concerning how things are done can present some barriers to this mid-twenties age group. When one conflicts with their well-developed 'common-sense' world view, one may get discouraged or penalized. For example: "Don't bring that new boyfriend home." (Or "don't make waves" in the company). This group may also be used to responding rapidly to well-codified and unambiguous signals. (Such as the comment "all the ladies in the Bridge Club disapproved when Mary's daughter ran off with the postman," or similar comments.) The speaker may respond too fast to allow internalization through absorption to occur—that theirs is a different story being presented by a younger/newer generation person.

Information may enter from the outside however, when the younger person tells the doubters stories about friends who did things differently or got engaged to different people. This shows adaptations of young women and men doing new kinds of things and dating new kinds of people—even those from another country or another part of this country. It scales this coding to a more abstract, broader and more diffused perspective. Brainstorming new friends, new trips, or other kinds of new activities like academic graduate courses, can give local gossip and grandmother's Bridge Club a new topic or slant for conversation.

According to Boisot (1998) in his book *Knowledge Assets,* knowledge can be fed in to the process, but that doesn't mean it ever will be fully objectively received, even by enhancing the understanding of intelligent people. Building the link between codification and complexity can be very convoluted and slow and takes time for the speaker to see the new information being received and understood.

One can ask:

Is the message received in the same way the message was sent?
Is the message received and understood?
Is the message acted upon as it was intended?

These things take time and the speaker may receive no feedback for a while. It's important to remember that people don't talk much when they are changing attitudes, however. These stages that are far-from-equilibrium feel chaotic, and are called 'dissipative' by the literature. This is not a comfortable state to be in. (See Figure 2.2 The Knowledge Cycle).

Sometimes spotting new patterns in "generally available information" is possible. For young adults: 'what other new things do their parents like?' might be a question to mention and to think about. As an 'order' appears the new behaviors or innovations one is trying out, seem less new.

Slowly two or three alternatives surface: get one's own apartment or townhouse—with or without roommates. One looks for a more career enhancing job, checks out Masters Degrees, and perhaps finds a more reliable car. One also begins to see relationships between alternatives. In researching these options one at a time, some answers begin to emerge. In finding their own place to live, decorating it in their own taste becomes possible. Stripes on the wall? A fuchsia accent wall? A zebra striped rug? Only one (or two if there's a roomate) people have a vote. Narrowing the search for a graduate degree to what is affordable and local or at least regional or accessible online, helps clarify that option. Researching jobs that might pay for graduate work, is seeing a relationship between two alternatives and gives this survey a new parameter.

At last one or more clarification emerges and one can start on how to "present the story" of decisions one is making. For dating it might be "I'm on sabbatical from relationships." For a job it might be finding hidden benefits in the job presently held. Making sense of life in these years becomes clearer or a least more explainable as some effort in foraging and research begins to result in sensemaking and making sense.

One person in this period of life said "Everyone knows what's best for me" adding that this chaos was made worse by being an only child, and the only girl on one side of the family, as well as being the youngest grandchild. Continuing, she said "I think differently than a lot of my friends. What they see or how they interpret things seems juvenile and even stupid to me. And then they tell me what they think I should do. One friend quit her job and cheats on her boyfriend but feels free to give me advice." "But usually things turn out the way I thought."

"The family thinks my current boyfriend is 'beneath' me. (Meaning differences in educational and income level, it seems.) This interrupts my own decision making. This is the most tumultuous time in my life regarding the decisions I have to make." "From all the jobs and all the courses I've had, I've learned what I don't want, but not what I do want!" My family is proud that I have a job, I have my own place and I'm self-reliant, but the family doesn't understand WHY I want this and not immediate marriage and children. "It all creates an unhealthy apathy in me; a resentment and an unwillingness to listen."

"I may be 25 but people are so willing to give me opinions and advice. Too many say now to abide by all the old social norms—and are shocked that I'm not in a serious relationship, not married, and/or not in graduate school." "But I have learned to define myself as I want and I feel secure," she added. She found this Sense-making chart and concept very helpful "because all day I'm supposed to look like I have it all together but at night I know I don't." "I thought I was the only one—all the others in their middle twenties did have their lives together." This was spoken by a number of those in their mid-twenties.

At thirty these mid-twenty years may seem like a memory—like eighth grade. One person's older brother at 29 ½ finished his Bachelors degree, got a job, and got married. He looked great at thirty!

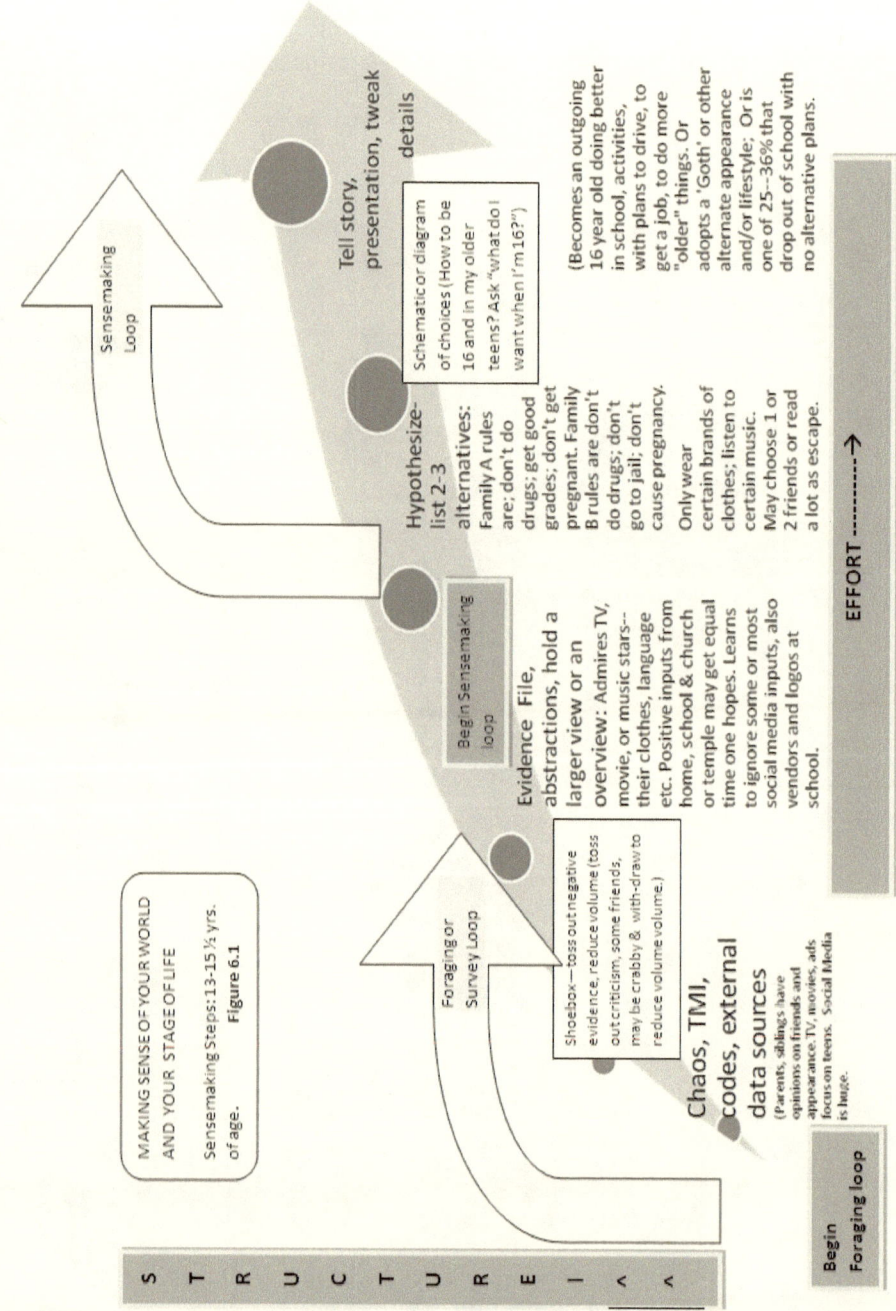

MAKING SENSE OF YOUR WORLD AND YOUR STAGE OF LIFE

Sensemaking Steps: 13-15 ½ yrs. of age.

Figure 6.1

Sensemaking Loop

Foraging or Survey Loop

Chaos, TMI, codes, external data sources

(Parents, siblings have opinions on friends and appearance. TV, movies, ads focus on teens. Social Media is huge.)

Evidence File, abstractions, hold a larger view or an overview: Admires TV, movie, or music stars-- their clothes, language etc. Positive inputs from home, school & church or temple may get equal time one hopes. Learns to ignore some or most social media inputs, also vendors and logos at school.

Shoebox-- toss out negative evidence, reduce volume (toss out criticism, some friends, may be crabby & with-draw to reduce volume volume.)

Begin Sensemaking loop

Hypothesize-- list 2-3 alternatives: Family A rules are; don't do drugs; get good grades; don't get pregnant. Family B rules are don't do drugs; don't go to jail; don't cause pregnancy.

Only wear certain brands of clothes; listen to certain music.

May choose 1 or 2 friends or read a lot as escape.

Schematic or diagram of choices (How to be 16 and in my older teens? Ask "what do I want when I'm16?")

Tell story, presentation, tweak details

(Becomes an outgoing 16 year old doing better in school, activities, with plans to drive, to get a job, to do more "older" things. Or adopts a 'Goth' or other alternate appearance and/or lifestyle; Or is one of 25--36% that drop out of school with no alternative plans.

EFFORT -------→

STRUCTURE IVV

Begin Foraging loop

44

Chapter 6

TMI Around Ages
13 to 15 1/2 Years of Age

The Too Much Information (TMI) era has definitely impacted the middle teen years in the Knowledge Era/Information Age, especially around age fifteen. This has always been a transition period as the teen may be nearly full grown physically and intellectually quite competent, but emotionally and socially he or she is not "together" yet, as parents know all too well. The inner structures for outer pressures are not in place yet related to brain development as they and all children are building their own brain "software". A good description and an aid to understanding the fifteen year old available from websites like www.homelearning.org says that it may seem that the expansive fourteen-year-old will get better and better as he or she turns fifteen, but the growth cycle hands out another inward cycle at fifteen. To see alternate cycles one can start with a look at age 13.

Understanding the Thirteen Year Old

Many new phases of behavior begin to emerge in the thirteen-year-old during this inward or internalized year. Thirteen-year-olds worry a lot and then say, "I worry about worrying." One thirteen year old was reassured to have this read to him from a book and said, "I do that!" This worrying is usually a normal sign of growth and leads to self-insight. Because so much happens for the first time during this year, time for internal processing is needed. He or she is not really withdrawing, but is probing into reality more deeply by turning things over in his or her mind. A thirteen-year-old may look sullen and glum without being either. A thirteen-year-old is reflective but more cooperative than at twelve. He or she may be less spontaneous or out-going. There is less conversation or humor. Sometimes a response is just a shrug. However, a thirteen-year-old is a tremendous self-critic.

Thirteen-year-old behavior includes getting along with siblings better than at eleven or twelve, except those between six and eleven. They have a constant expenditure of newfound energy on private projects and voracious reading, as one way to satisfy an inner urge for new ideas and thoughts.

They show extreme busyness that leaves little time for all he or she wants to do, much less for household chores. They are friendly, but not communicative or spontaneous. They are better able to control anger than at eleven or twelve and show a well-established appetite, and for some it's still as large as the twelve-year-old appetite. They are going to bed earlier, but need parents to remind him or her to turn off the lights, iPod, texting, computer or radio. They are caring for hair more than fingernails and toenails, boys more than girls.

They now are surer of likes and dislikes and are capable of buying all but major purchases. They may have a room that is cluttered not only with clothes and books, but also with papers and dishes from left over snacks on the floor, but are now carrying through with chores with a certain amount of willingness. They enjoy cooking, possibly breakfast on the weekend or deserts from mixes. Thirteen is beginning to see him or herself more clearly. He or she has good insight and understands what another person means.

The thirteen-year-old needs parents that understand when he or she says, "I'm not too good-natured." Another said "I became reclusive" in a family with some problems and changes. They also need parents that don't mind not knowing how to approach him or her when he or she snaps back with one-word answers, and parents that also leave him or her alone to allow time for ruminating or cogitating on the day's events (or whatever). They need love and affection, but not in public, as thirteen is often embarrassed by his or her mother or father. A parent that is tactful and reasonable with him or her in a grown-up way, staying on the surface, is desired. (Thirteens don't understand their own depths too well).

In dealing with these ages of kids, parents can ask them: "On a scale of 1 to 10 why don't you want to do this?" When they answer, ask them, "why isn't the number lower?" Their answer helps the child clarify reasons about what it is he or she *wants* to do about this concern or issue (Pink, 2012). They do well with parents that support a wide range of hobbies, activities and interests; the happy result is less time spent in front of the television or computer screen or on the iPhone.

Understanding the Fourteen Year Old

At fourteen the withdrawal, shyness and touchiness of the thirteen-year-old give way to an open, expansive personality phase with more laughter, noise and singing in the home. A fourteen year-old is better oriented to both him or herself and to the surrounding environment. Fourteen enjoys life and feels the pressures of mounting energy. A fourteen-year-old has a more mature attitude towards adults in general and to his or her family in particular, but still can be hypercritical. However, he or she is much less subjective than at thirteen, and has more friends.

Fourteen-year-old behavior includes developing new capacities to understand how other people feel and fighting with siblings verbally rather than physically. Their behavior includes being sensitive to group standards with friends; but devotion to a group may go to extremes and may be in competition with concrete demands of home and school. They have eager, tireless communication with friends, especially on the telephone, or on Skype or on their mobile phone—especially with texting. They show energy, expansiveness, exuberance, but can become swamped with undertakings and activities. There is a new tendency to be realistic and objective, on the other hand, with a willingness to look at two sides of a question. They are beginning to use their minds in new ways, as abstract thinking develops. They are happy and self-reliant, but also self-critical, using these new powers of reasoning.

They have newly crossed over towards more physical maturity, with rapid height growth for boys, and the body form of a young woman for girls. There is continuing enjoyment of eating; they have a loud voice; but now know enough to go to bed and also hang up their clothes—most of the time.

They are very aware of outward appearance, especially his or her complexion. Parents see them being more of a spendthrift than in the past but they have a changed attitude towards work. The fourteen-year-old is easy going, but gets moody.

They now are worrying less than at thirteen, but still have pet worries. No longer pathetically edgy and touchy, the fourteen-year-old seems to be coming into his or her own as a person. His or her maturity level is somewhere between elementary school and senior high school. Emotionally the fourteen year old is not as precarious as last year, and has loosened up from the tight withdrawn ways of the thirteen-year-old. A fourteen-year-old with all his or her qualities of expansiveness, capacity for leadership and readiness for change, is thinking about the kind of world he or she would like to live in: a world with unity and peace, a better world in general, with a better chance for people to grow up. Indeed if everyone followed the vision they had at fourteen, the world might be a different place. In fact, career-planning consultants encourage people to think back to their dreams and ideas of these 13 to 14 year-old years.

Fourteen-year-olds need to be helped to bring to full realization their promising potentials, and parents that understand the fuller impact of how much it costs to raise a child. They would like parents who accept an apology after a sharp word is spoken. They also need help in understanding how their activities relate to their whole lives. For instance parents can say, "You'll probably enjoy ice skating your whole life," etc. As always they need love, affection and understanding perhaps expressed by a hand on the arm or shoulder (when in public).

Understanding the Fifteen Year Old

Around 15 he or she may seem apathetic and sleepy, if not actually lazy. This seeming appearance, however, covers inner thinking about new experiences and inner states of feelings. A new capacity to focus on details of thought and feeling characterizes the fifteen-year-old.

Figure 6.2
(by M.A.J. age 15)

One fifteen said of this illustration "This is really true!" Many make a noticeable effort to find just the right words to express themselves correctly. Texting is pervasive and popular as it allows one to check words before sending them. Concern with the minute and for precision replaces the expansiveness of fourteen and precedes the integration that comes at sixteen. He or she has a thoughtful, quiet, serious side that is in evidence.

The behavior of a fifteen-year-old includes:

- Showing new sensibilities, irritations, resistances, aversions and suspicions, showing a new self awareness and perceptiveness.
- Omitting or skimping on greetings to family members.
- Resisting restraints or restrictions, no matter how reasonable.
- Engaging parents in a cold war, which varies in degree, despite feelings of loyalty.
- Slamming the door when leaving, especially when getting out at night; following an urge for independence.
- Being affected by the pressures of groups.
- Being gregarious and liking groups, except those at home; wanting to outgrow parental control, but feeling conflicted about this.
- Better relations with siblings, "seeing" an improvement in the siblings.
- Feeling a gnawing anguish if mother and father do not get along with each other.
- Sinking into a slump when the effort required defining thoughts and feelings is too great; unfortunately this can lead to school drop-out.
- Revealing new interests and hidden talents in reactions to specialized courses and activities at school.
- Being neither anti-school or anti-home—just needs time to mull things over and organize him or herself internally.
- Showing an ability to identify with other people and situations.
- Loving an argument and dispute for its own sake.
- Having a low threshold for all sorts of stimuli (e.g., everything bothers him or her).
- Calming down on the subject of clothes.
- Having emotions like the weather, sunny and gloomy; having times feeling very tired, discouraged and mixed up.
- Not getting as mad as often as he or she used to.
- Reminiscing about the fears he or she used to have, and about other earlier stages of development. Better yet, he or she may reminisce at sixteen about fifteen.
- Needing to maintain an apartness, by withdrawing internally or going to the bedroom, becoming secretive, defensive, not wanting parents to know about his or her activities (no matter how reasonable).

☐ Wanting to think that parents "don't really have the upper hand". Not being the easiest person to teach in school, but learns quickly in new fields. Finding that relaxation and sleeping mean a lot to him or her. A fifteen year old wants to define his or her thoughts, philosophy and place in life. There is a constant cry for liberty and independence (even though he or she may have had these!). He or she is expert at stalling in answers to questions and ends up telling the questioner as little as possible.

Security is important to the fifteen year old and he or she wishes it for his or herself, family and the whole world. He or she is down to earth in his or her thinking, revisiting concepts from ages nine and ten. Since fifteen has a tendency to rebel against authority, even though confused and floundering his or herself, how authority treats him or her is very important. Some of his or her most annoying comments need to be ignored. Real leaders often emerge at fifteen.

A fifteen-year-old needs:

☐ Time to become receptive to requests and questions, his or her answers may come slowly.
☐ Parents that are aware that he or she may be arguing for "fun", but also to get his or her point across. Some teens stubbornly maintain a closed mind.
☐ To not be idle; he or she would rather be rushed than do nothing.
☐ To have parents and teachers understand that he or she is uncertain and searching, with much turmoil and depth to this inner disquietude.
☐ Parents that understand there are times when he or she wants his or her feelings to be known; one doesn't have to be a genius to figure out the meaning of the cold stare, the shuffled walk, the apathy and quietness.
☐ Love, patience, and kindness to carry him or her through this inner cycle to the greater integration that emerges at sixteen.

(Adapted from Gesell and Ilg, *Youth: The Years from Ten to Sixteen*)

The sensemaking that a fifteen-year-old is going through can seem overwhelming with so much internal reflecting to do, plus constant bombardment from being a focus of the media world in TV, movies, social networking and advertising. Add to this the usual "improvement" comments and criticism from parents, friends, relatives and even siblings, plus a growth spurt, and *chaos and TMI* (too much information) result. (Italics are the stages on the Sensemaking chart Figure 6.1).

Figure 6.3
(2013 by M.A.J., age 15)

In a need to reduce this volume or *"shoebox"* it and to toss out negative evidence, some teens just shut down or withdraw, and most get crabby. As they develop more mental abilities to *make abstractions and hold a larger view* some settle on celebrities to copy in their clothes, appearance and even language. The intellectual abilities of this age group can be impressive and the home, school and church or temple have opportunities for inputs, activities and trips which build their *Evidence File.* Building values needs to continue through these years, even if there is not much positive feedback.

In *listing two or three alternatives* some families have brief, simple and clear rules that teens can quote back. In Family A, the daughter is told: Don't do drugs; get good grades; and don't get pregnant. Family B with three sons has a similar but different list: Don't do drugs; don't get put in jail; and don't cause a pregnancy.

These and other teens clarify their Chaos sometimes, by settling on certain brands or types of clothing or types of music. They are re-defining themselves from Middle School to be a high school student and later a high school graduate.

Figure 6.4
(2013 by M.A.J., age 15)

Some realize that there are clear 'choices' about "how do I want to be?" as they become old enough to get jobs and to drive, they realize they are recognized by the "grown-up" world and do not have to resort to smoking, drinking and sex to prove that they are grown up.

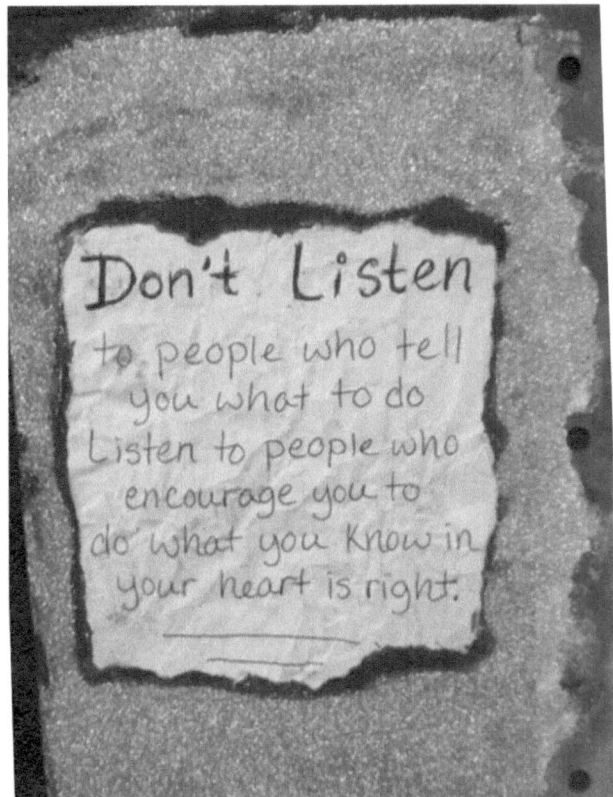

Figure 6.5
(2013 M.A.J)

In *Presenting the Story* some teens continue with a strong self image and are able to plan for college and/or career and move forward. Some adopt an alternate life style and appearance. Today 25% to 36% are dropping out of high school without a long range plan or knowledge about spending sixty to eighty years without the benchmark of a college degree. Some are hobbled by poverty and/or disability and must work to help support their family.

Schools could help with new 'out-of-the-box' alternative and flex-time classes in the evening, or in early and late afternoons for working students. Physical and behavior problem students could do more alone with online courses, even at the public library for access to computers. New ways of finding technology to help with this high drop-out rate are needed.

The onslaught of "too much (commercial) information" on an age group that is not mentally, emotionally and ethically strong, has taken a toll and now some regions have one in three students dropping out of high school. As the Knowledge Era progresses, some knowledge era solutions are needed to address this challenge.

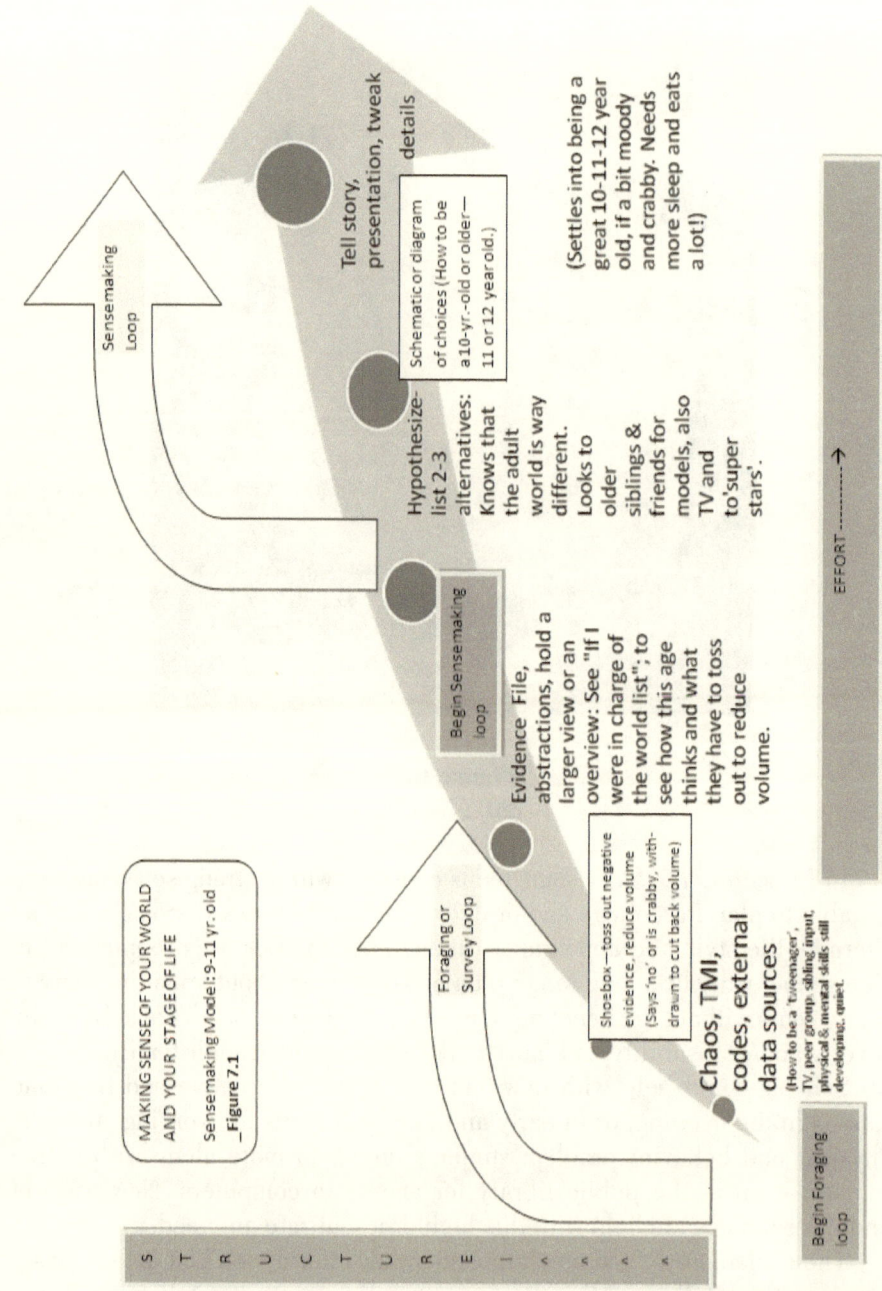

MAKING SENSE OF YOUR WORLD AND YOUR STAGE OF LIFE

Sensemaking Model: 9-11 yr. old

_Figure 7.1

Sensemaking Loop

Foraging or Survey Loop

Chaos, TMI, codes, external data sources

(How to be a 'tweenager', TV, peer group sibling input, physical & mental skills still developing, quiet.

Begin Foraging loop

Shoebox—toss out negative evidence, reduce volume (Says 'no' or is crabby, withdrawn to cut back volume)

Begin Sensemaking loop

Evidence File, abstractions, hold a larger view or an overview: See "If I were in charge of the world list"; to see how this age thinks and what they have to toss out to reduce volume.

Hypothesize-list 2-3 alternatives: Knows that the adult world is way different. Looks to older siblings & friends for models, also TV and to 'super stars'.

Schematic or diagram of choices (How to be a 10-yr.-old or older— 11 or 12 year old.)

Tell story, presentation, tweak details

(Settles into being a great 10-11-12 year old, if a bit moody and crabby. Needs more sleep and eats a lot!)

EFFORT -------->

S T R U C T U R E | ^ ^ ^

54

Chapter 7

TMI and the Nine to Eleven Year Old

An 11 ½ year old who is growing fast, receives TMI (Too Much Information) about what it means to be teenager or 'tweenager' from movies, TV shows, video games, hand-held electronics, friends and even from books. They feel stretched and overwhelmed and sometimes just blow up at parents or siblings. One child development book (Gesell) said this age gets along with everyone in the family except those between ages 5 and 10. The mother of one child said to him "I'm sorry, dear, that's all we have in the family." Numerous interviews over several years showed that this age gets along best with other 11 ½ and 12 ½ year olds. The problem is they ARE growing up physically, sometimes growing between four and six inches in a year. Listening to elevens and twelves talking to each other, one hears "I don't want to grow up"—"I want to grow up" and one can hear how ambivalent and torn they are.

Some children reduce the volume of information coming in by being crabby and withdrawing to their rooms. When one looks at a listing that an almost-nine-year-old wrote in response to *"What would it be like if you were in charge of the world?"* school exercise, the answers are great and show an active imagination!

If I were in charge of the world, I would cancel long lines, bees, and mosquitoes.

If I were in charge of the world, there would be more flowers, trees, and chocolate.

If I were in charge of the world, you wouldn't have dentists, shots, an braces.

If I were in charge of the world, ice cream would be a vegetable.

And sometimes when a person who forgot to clean and accidentally forgot to do homework—could still be in charge of the world.

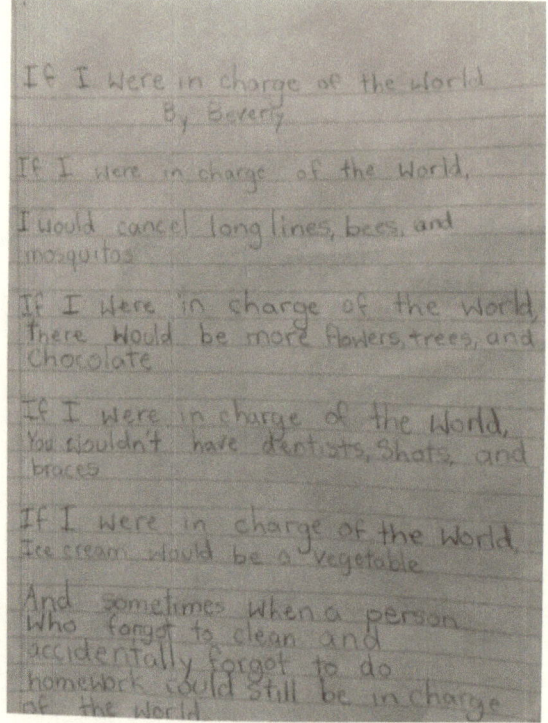

Figure 7.2 "If I Were in Charge of the World"
(2012, B.J.L.)

One can see how this age thinks, but the child is often embarrassed to have adults and older siblings know too much about these cherished views. Certainly this child never wants siblings to know and tease her about them. This chart graphic shows just a small part of the volume of ideas and thoughts that this age is sorting through and reducing to a manageable amount in these growing years.

Understanding The Nine to Eleven Year Old

The nine year old moves on to the calm, balanced, flexible nature of a ten year old (plus or minus six months for a particular child), and gives way at eleven to a new growth force, eventually to be called adolescence. Many tokens of the growing up process begin to emerge. As with two-and-a-half and age 15, a period of relative calm at 2, 10, and 14 is followed by instability, mood swings, lack of flexibility and what is generally a stage of turmoil.

The emotions of an eleven year old rise with swift crescendos and have peaks of intensity. Bursts of laughter, yelling, and rudeness can cause endless irritation. This age is in a state of change and is "breaking up" from the smoothness of childhood to allow room for growth into adulthood. In another decade this child will be at the edge of maturity.

Parents often feel confused and frustrated by the intense behavior they see, so different from the year before. Often the child does not understand it either and appreciates patience from parents (which, however, is rarely acknowledged).

The eleven year old behavior includes:

- v   Incessant bodily activity and energy expenditure.
- v   Constant eating, talking, and sleeping (but often a growth spurt doesn't really show until the next year for boys). Some have a "fat" period. Many eat steadily after school, take a break for dinner, and then continue their snacks.
- v   Developing strength and the beginnings of sexual maturation.
- v   Dissatisfaction with bedtime, regardless of its time—although needing sleep and peevish without it.
- v   Hating work and resisting doing it—good at making up excuses.
- v   Having odd, vague, uncomfortable emotional feelings.
- v   More ability to challenge than to respond to parents.
- v   Willingness to be helpful "when he or she is in the mood", but doesn't want a parent to yell at him or her or be critical. ("They can dish it out but they can't take it") one parent said.
- v   A lack of capability in answering parents demands.
- v   Getting on better with one parent than the other.
- v   Arguing about everything, strenuous self-assertiveness.
- v   Not being into abstract thinking yet—things have to be concrete for them to really understand.

It is not easy to understand the laws of growth and development at this particular stage, but eleven year olds need:

- v   Time, patience, and understanding. Parents who realize that this is less personal rebellion against them than a reaction to complexities and uncertainties inside the child. Not too much lenience or too much sensitivity.
- v   An atmosphere conducive to good growth—but the child must do his or her own growing.
- v   A full refrigerator and adequate sleep.
- v   Good humor, fairness, affection, and interesting activities. Reassurance that "we'll get through this together" without probing inner depths which the child doesn't understand either.

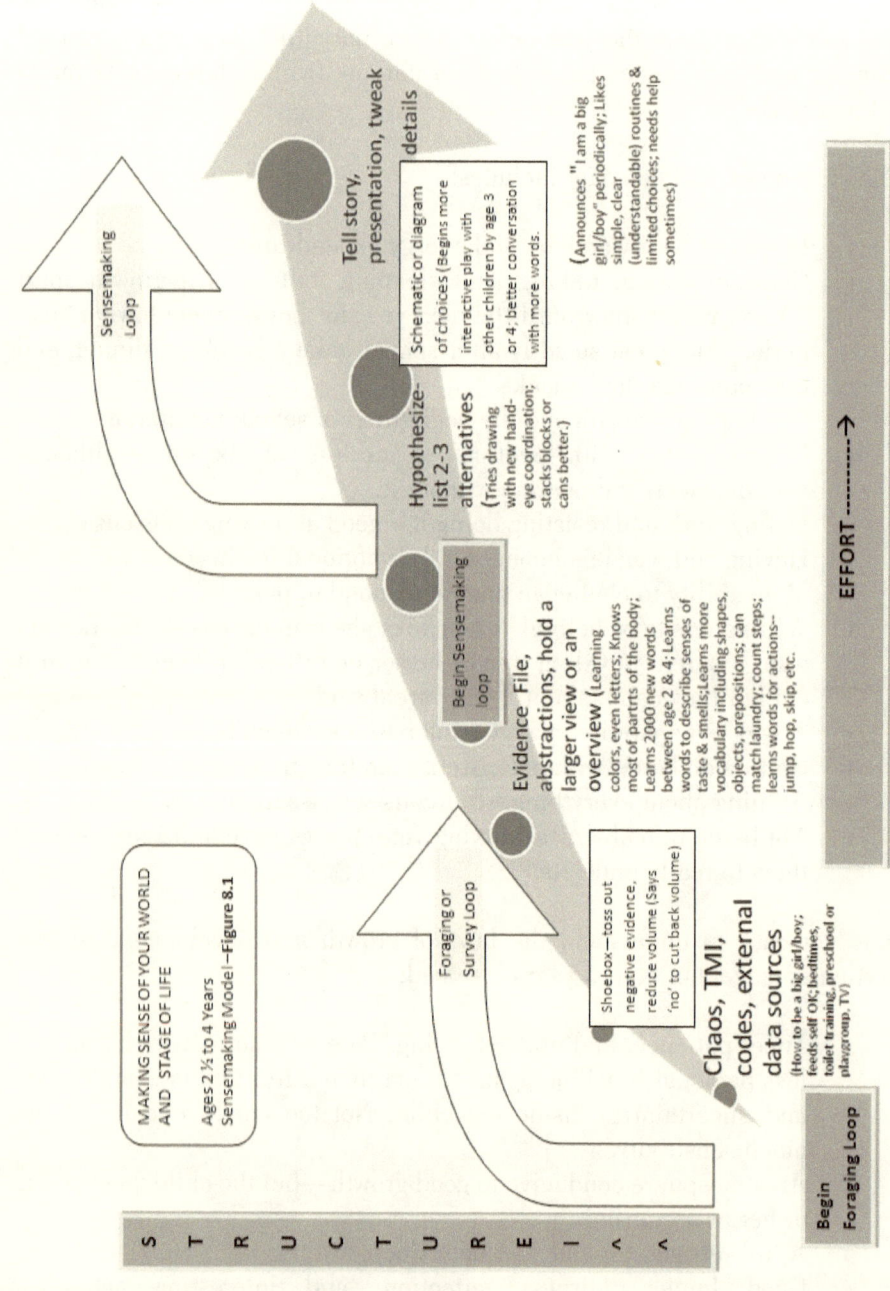

MAKING SENSE OF YOUR WORLD AND STAGE OF LIFE

Ages 2½ to 4 Years
Sensemaking Model—Figure 8.1

Chaos, TMI, codes, external data sources

(How to be a big girl/boy; feeds self OK; bedtimes, toilet training, preschool or playgroup, TV)

Shoebox—toss out negative evidence. reduce volume (Says 'no' to cut back volume)

Begin Foraging Loop

Foraging or Survey Loop

Evidence File, abstractions, hold a larger view or an overview (Learning colors, even letters; Knows most of partrts of the body; Learns 2000 new words between age 2 & 4; Learns words to describe senses of taste & smells;Learns more vocabulary including shapes, objects, prepositions; can match laundry; count steps; learns words for actions— jump, hop, skip, etc.

Begin Sensemaking loop

Hypothesize- list 2-3 alternatives (Tries drawing with new hand-eye coordination; stacks blocks or cans better.)

Sensemaking Loop

Tell story, presentation, tweak details

Schematic or diagram of choices (Begins more interactive play with other children by age 3 or 4; better conversation with more words.

(Announces "I am a big girl/boy periodically; Likes simple, clear (understandable) routines & limited choices; needs help sometimes)

EFFORT ------>

S T R U C T U R E   I V V

Chapter 8

TMI at Two and a Half Years Old Up to Four Years Old

Too much information comes at young children from all angles and they ARE growing up. Think of a two-and-a-half-year-old child told to be a "big girl" (or "big boy"). The child isn't sure what a "big girl/boy" is, but is sure he/she doesn't know how. So the child clings to wearing diapers and refusing to be toilet trained or to another babyish behavior.

If one looks at the steps in the Sensemaking model as applied to two and three year olds, they become clearer. Two to three year olds still can't talk too well, so they have trouble explaining their ambivalence and frustration. Some are willing to try new things. Some see a friend their age (or even younger) who is toilet trained or who has given up "baby talk". The child can then hypothesize new ways to act, but will swing back and forth. Accidents do happen. Finally they settle into a "mostly trained and mostly acting older mode and become more like a pre-schooler than a toddler—and by now they can talk better. The child is entering a "re-codification" for new 'codes' needed for the new age they're becoming in this Sensemaking loop. Some children with these behaviors become very secure and are very popular in middle school, but were slow to survey and try out being older before they understood it well enough, to "see" it for themselves. Some children just have a longer *"foraging loop"*.

As can be seen in the Sensemaking Chart for Two-to-Four Year-Olds, much "external data" is coming at a child this age: bedtimes, feeding themselves (which they do pretty well with much interest!), toilet training, playgroups and the preschool. Modeling behavior from television or DVDs yields more information. Mostly a child this age plays alone better than with others, followed by 'parallel play,' and starts interacting more with other children with co-operative play as language improves. In fact many of these routines improve as vocabulary and language improve, especially helping the toilet training.

Two's are famous for saying "no" as they have a very short circuit breaker, but also this device helps *reduce* the volume of new information coming in. As they look around and see children close to their age trying new things, they begin to hold a larger view that "maybe I can do this". At the same time they are learning colors and numbers, learning words to describe the senses, especially taste and smell. The child learns 2,000 words between ages two and four including much needed prepositions and directions like "in" "out" "up" "down" "across" "in front of" "in back of". New words for actions like "jump" "hop" and "skip" become second nature and are needed in the Kindergarten Readiness screening. A Vietnamese manicurist said her son came home from preschool with a new word "hope". She showed us with a hop and I explained the word "hop" and the different spelling and meaning of it than "hope". This young child was teaching this Asian family his new words.

As the child develops he or she begins to see two or three alternatives to behaviors: like "try it like Mary" did. Also shouting "MY turn" appears. The new choices include playing more with other children and better conversations. Tantrums are less frequent, but loud when they occur.

As their "story" clarifies, they present it periodically with "I am a big girl" or "I am a big boy". A simple clear routine with understandable and limited choices helps this preschooler continue to move forward.

Understanding Twos, Threes and Fours

General Characteristics of the Two-Year-Old include that he/she: Demonstrates unevenly developed motor skills. Large muscle coordination is good (the child can walk and climb), but small muscles and eye-hand coordination are still not well developed. He or she gradually acquires skills in dressing and feeding him or herself. The child goes through rapid language development at this age. Vocabulary increases from a few words or short sentences to up to 2,000 words by age four as mentioned above. The child also goes through changes in sleep patterns. He or she is gradually giving up daytime naps, but as mentioned above still needs a rest period and about 12 hours of sleep at night and has almost a complete set of baby teeth. She or he often has begun to establish toilet habits and usually will be able to handle his or her own needs by age four.

However characteristic behavior includes that he or she: Plays alone, or plays beside, but not with, others; Does not share or take turns too well; Often says "no," but gradually becomes able to accept adult limits. Wants adult approval and likes to be close to mother and father.

The good news is that the child wants to help around the house and is beginning to understand his or her surroundings and the demands of daily life. He or she likes to feel familiar with things and have a sense of security, to balance the "too much information" of growing up. Thus this age imitates language, manners, and habits and is constantly active and then shows tiredness by becoming irritable or restless. She and especially he seems to have an urgent need to explore, but gradually learns what is acceptable and what is not. Much repetition is important. The child demonstrates great curiosity and asks countless questions.

This child has a special need for love and affection from parents. Two-year-olds also need guidance and a pattern of behavior to follow and have a need for time, patience, understanding, and genuine interest from adults. They need simple, clear routines and limited choices but also have a need for opportunities to learn sharing and taking turns, to learn to play cooperatively with other children.

Understanding Three-Year-Olds

Every child is different, as every parent knows. Still, it is helpful to know what other children might be doing developmentally at a particular age. If the child doesn't fit this particular age group, look at material on six months older or children in your area or elsewhere. By discovering more about general stages of child development, one may be able to better understand the child's everyday behavior as well as his or her occasional behavior. Did you know that the parent is the child's most important teacher? Research has shown this repeatedly; research also shows that the most important thing for a child's success is for an adult to think he or she is wonderful.

General Characteristics of the Three-Year-Old include that he or she demonstrates motor skills that are still unevenly developed. Large muscle coordination is still much better than small muscle and eye-hand coordination, and the child has a full set of baby teeth. The child shows an awareness of the sequence of steps and the probable outcomes of his or her activities. The three-year-old begins to plan ahead. He or she continues to develop language ability at full speed. The most important and amazing verbal development occurs this year and the child acquires more skills in feeding and dressing him or herself. This age child goes through changes in sleep patterns, but still needs a daytime nap or rest period and nearly 12 hours of sleep at night. A three-year-old may get tired easily but toilet habits are getting better.

Characteristic Behaviors include that he or she shows more interest in playing with other children. He or she still needs to play alone some, and is not ready to share or take turns *too* often. They want adult approval and like to cuddle. The three-year-old may reject the adult, but still needs him or her. This child is even more interested in helping around the house and likes to imitate language, manners, and habits. He or she will experiment and explore within adult limits and gradually learns what is acceptable behavior and what is not.

They enjoy looking at picture and story books, and have a better understanding of words. A three-year-old shows great curiosity and asks many question

This age child has special needs for the security of love and affection from parents, adult direction, and a consistent pattern of behavior to follow. He or she has a need for time, patience, understanding, and genuine interest from adults, and a need for simple, clear daily schedules and limited choices. They also have a need for opportunities to learn give-and-take, and to play with other children and a need for a wider scope of activities.

Understanding Four-Year-Olds

Every child is different, as every parent knows. Still, it is helpful to know what other children might be doing developmentally at a particular age. If the child doesn't fit his or her particular age group, read the material about younger children here or look for material about six months older children. By finding out more about the general stages of child development, one may be better able to understand the child's everyday behavior as well as his or her occasional behavior.

Did you know that the parent is a child's most important teacher? Research has shown this over and over; research also shows that the most important thing for a child's success and achievement is for an adult to think he or she is wonderful, which can't be said too many times.

General Characteristics of the Four-Year-Old include that he or she has the desire to run, not walk, and the desire to yell, not talk. However, a four-year-old still wants adult approval. His or her motor development is still better in terms of large muscles than small muscles or eye-hand coordination. There is rapid language development which continues up to and past 2,000 words. This child becomes quite skillful in feeding and dressing him or herself, but may need occasional help and develops sleep patterns that still need to incorporate up to 12 hours of sleep each night. Toilet habits are established. The four-year-old child usually takes care of his or her own needs by this age period.

Characteristic Behaviors of this age child include that he or she shows more independence and reliability. The child has more interests in many things, including an interest in people and the way they act. He or she also plays with real purpose, and engages in much more imaginative play. He or she begins to pretend to be other people or animals. This child better understands his or her environment and enjoys trips. He or she asks searching questions about people and their relationships to others. He or she is able to accept necessary limits and restraints from adults, but likes to be close to mother and father.

Again this child is constantly active, likes to help around the house, and imitates language and habits. He or she becomes capable of longer stretches of quiet activity as he or she approaches five and learns many new words and asks many questions.

This age Child has special needs for love and affection from parents. Four-year-olds also need guidance and a pattern of behavior they can imitate. They need to feel valued. They need time, patience, understanding, and genuine interest from adults. They especially need a wider scope of activity and limited freedom to move about, and to visit away from the home surroundings and have a need for opportunities to do things.

Gradually this child enters the "balanced" age of five defined as 'when he or she can handle most of the things he/she aspires to do'. A calmer, happier age emerges at age five. Their story is easier to present.

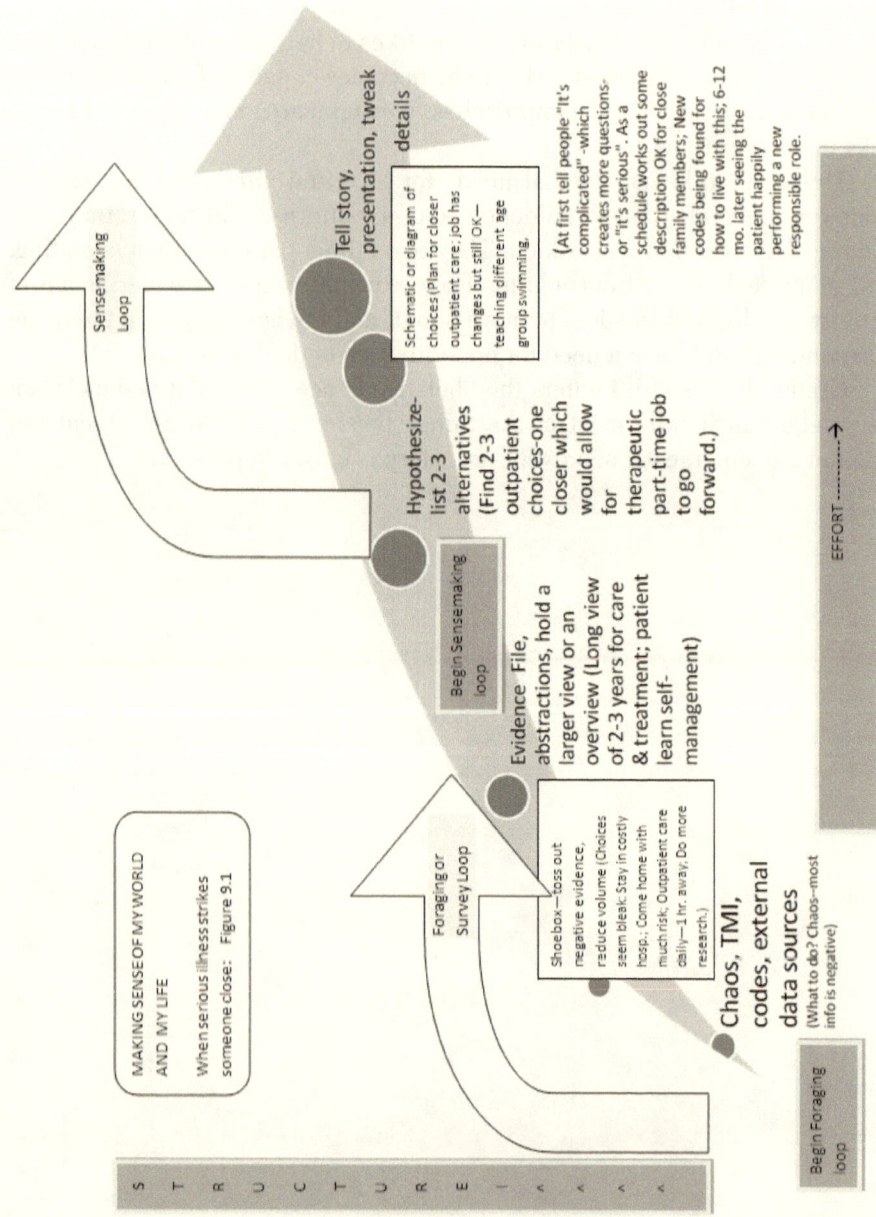

MAKING SENSE OF MY WORLD AND MY LIFE

When serious illness strikes someone close: Figure 9.1

Sensemaking Loop

Foraging or Survey Loop

Begin Sensemaking loop

Begin Foraging loop

S T R U C T U R E   I N   v   v   v

EFFORT ⟶

Chaos, TMI, codes, external data sources
(What to do? Chaos—most info is negative)

Shoebox—toss out negative evidence, reduce volume (Choices seem bleak: Stay in costly hosp.; Come home with much risk; Outpatient care daily—1 hr. away; Do more research.)

Evidence File, abstractions, hold a larger view or an overview (Long view of 2-3 years for care & treatment; patient learn self-management)

Hypothesize-list 2-3 alternatives (Find 2-3 outpatient choices-one closer which would allow for therapeutic part-time job to go forward.)

Tell story, presentation, tweak details

Schematic or diagram of choices (Plan for closer outpatient care; job has changes but still OK—teaching different age group swimming.

(At first tell people "It's complicated" –which creates more questions– or "it's serious". As a schedule works out some description OK for close family members; New codes being found for how to live with this; 6-12 mo. later seeing the patient happily performing a new responsible role.

Chapter 9

Making Sense in Your Life:
When Serious Illness strikes
a Family Member

When serious illness strikes you or a family member, whether it be cancer, appendicitis, or some form of mental illness, a feeling of *chaos and too much information from external sources* results. A fairly clear cut path is available for well known issues such as appendicitis. However, with the many forms of cancer and of mental illness there is too much information (TMI) multiplied by past experience and stories one has heard from others.

A first step might be to *"shoebox"* this TMI and toss out negative evidence to reduce the volume. Most input is negative and that is scary. This is NOW not the past or someone else's experience—or their friend's. Today's medicine with medical information doubling every two to five years contains today's solutions. There is always hope.

In gathering an *evidence file* to try and hold a larger view, the choices may seem bleak, such as : 1) stay in a very expensive hospital; 2) come home with much risk, but this may be the patient's choice; 3) outpatient care daily, but it is one hour's drive away; 4) research more about closer outpatient care and resources that are more local.

As caretakers *hypothesize two or three alternatives* they find: 1) two or three alternatives such as more local radiation treatments; 2) this might allow for a therapeutic part-time job or even a full time job with flex hours or 3) in the case of a bone marrow transplant for a widow, a sister came and stayed with her; 4) these hours and arrangements allow treatment to go forward while being supportive to the person affected. In one or two situations like this a work place job was set up but it had changes in it. This was still okay in the schematic of choices with teaching or counseling a different age group or at a different location then had previously been the thought through.

In *telling the story and tweaking the details* there can be difficulty as people want to know more and are concerned, before adequate details are available and an adequate story may not even exist yet. Saying "it's complicated" or "it's serious" only generates more questions. As a schedule works out some description is possible for close family members. New "codes" are being formed for how to live with this, replacing the "chaos" feeling at the start. Hopefully in six to twelve months seeing the patient happily performing a new responsibility and role (such as a teenager driving, or a counselor counseling vocational students), rewards the research, waiting and adapting needed for a new perspective.

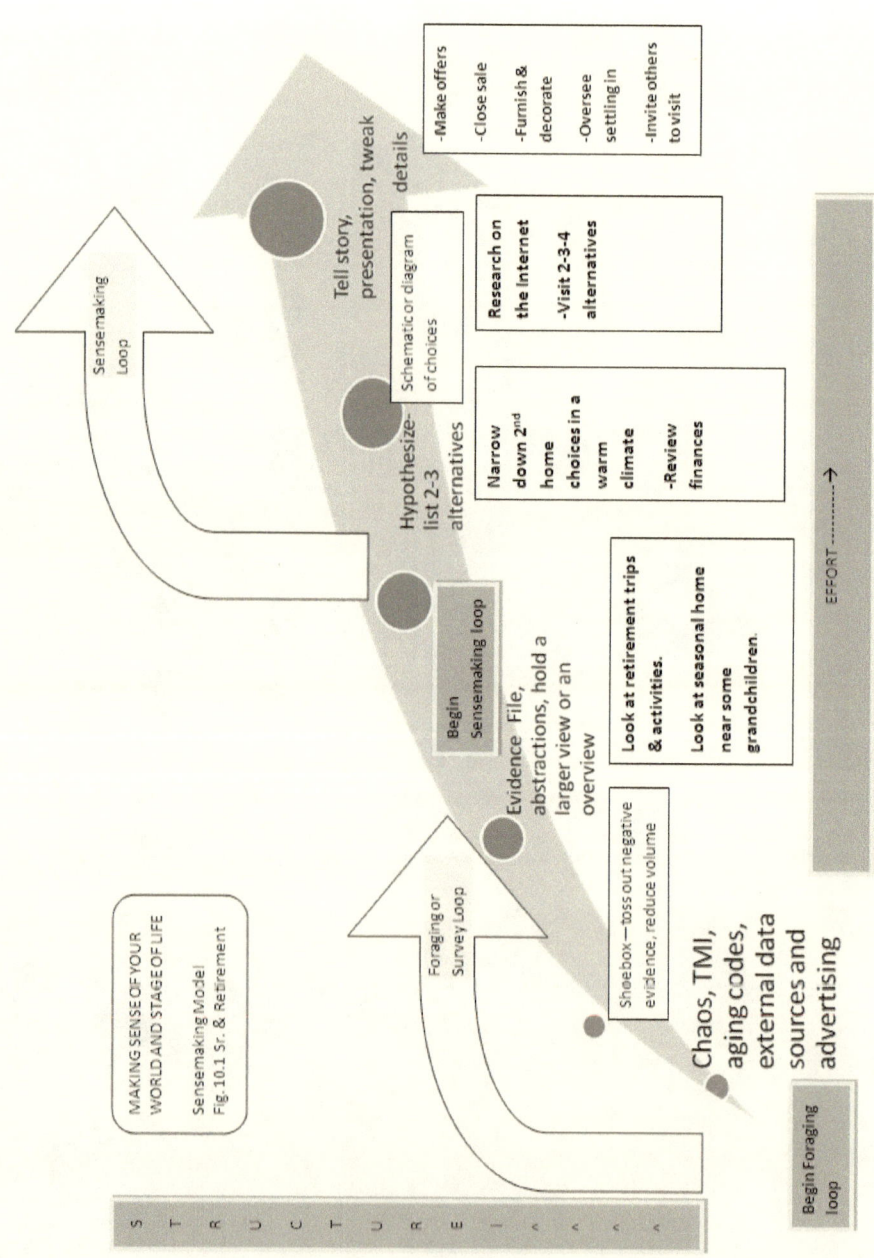

MAKING SENSE OF YOUR
WORLD AND STAGE OF LIFE

Sensemaking Model
Fig. 10.1 Sr. & Retirement

Sensemaking Loop

Foraging or Survey Loop

Tell story, presentation, tweak details

Schematic or diagram of choices

Research on the Internet
-Visit 2-3-4 alternatives

Hypothesize-list 2-3 alternatives

Narrow down 2nd home choices in a warm climate
-Review finances

Begin Sensemaking loop

Evidence File, abstractions, hold a larger view or an overview

Look at retirement trips & activities.
Look at seasonal home near some grandchildren.

Shoebox—toss out negative evidence, reduce volume

Chaos, TMI, aging codes, external data sources and advertising

-Make offers
-Close sale
-Furnish & decorate
-Oversee settling in
-Invite others to visit

EFFORT ------->

Begin Foraging loop

S T R U C T U R E ^ ^ ^

Chapter 10

Reinventing Yourself at Any Life Stage and Planning for Later Years

Reinventing Yourself at Any Life Stage

Around the ages of transitions after the late 20's people can find a life change dramatic enough to "require" reinventing themselves. (Periods before the late 20's are covered in earlier chapters.) The first feelings of chaos and too much information may be multiplied by codes, rules, and conventions of the region where they live clashing with very different codes or rules from a past residential locality. One person had moved to the east coast to a rural region, from Southern California and then changed jobs after several years. She felt the culture clash as chaos and too much information.

A first step in Sensemaking might be to *Shoebox* these codes into those needed from other times and places, to sort out what seems important in **this** place at **this** time. As *evidence* and a larger more abstract view become clearer, two or three alternatives will present themselves for further review and trial. Perhaps a college coaching career (this person's former role) can lead to working with youth and adolescents in other venues. Perhaps college faculty experience can lead to college administrative positions, particularly in Continuing Education with young adults. Coaching can then be added in a volunteer capacity.

In *hypothesizing* possible new choices, one can research availability of such positions locally and on the Internet. In preparing the story for possible presentation in the resume, the interviews and job applications, with or without a move of residence, one can research the new choices of institutions of education for their background and culture. Then send out applications.

Thinking about the time or place one set of codes or conventions may have been in place for yourself or for others versus the time and place now, another example can be seen with working mothers. They are told they should be home with their children. Stay-at-home Moms are told they should be working—the result being unsettled feelings about whichever choice has been made. A single woman may get the feeling she is 'supposed' to be married by her age. This is not a new problem and is addressed often by many others.

Whatever the case, one doesn't have to abide by the local codes, rules, norms and conventions or they can be adapted for the new, 'reinvented' self one is seeking. As in Figure 2.2 of the Knowledge Cycle, one can move from a diffused, chaotic state, to thinking and learning, and then moving beyond existing norms to a new knowledge state possibly with new codes, freely chosen.

Later Life, Aging Codes and Codification

In human development books the ages beyond retirement are often called: young old age, middle old-age, and old-old age. Recently this was updated to 'go-go', 'slow-go', and 'no-go'. Each stage is approximately 15 years long for each stage, generally starting with retirement from the full-time workplace. The young-old-age or 'go-go' period is characterized by taking trips and doing things that were put off while working and child raising. Middle-old-age or 'slow-go' has some health issues and symptoms but continues earlier patterns. Old-old age or 'no-go' may need assisted living and more traditional steps.

Taking the theories of Boisot (1998) and Petrolli and Card (1999), this writer suddenly realized the experience of buying a seasonal home fit the steps and explained the confusion! And furthermore it explained why she was publishing these details to "tell the story".

Step one of *chaos or 'too much information' and codification,* rules and conventions around and leading to the subject of "you're supposed to retire at a certain age" appeared. One's children may think so; and one's geographical region may think this in general, especially in rural areas. There is a pattern (or 'code') of how to act and be at this age and which can happen at other ages. (See Chapters 5 to 8).

Therefore one *surveys* the possibilities within this 'code': More activities in areas of one's interests; one tries new things and maybe takes some trips to prepare for stopping work. But the result may be that work is still going well but one is tired. This writer then checked out townhouses near one of her son's families in a warmer climate. She knew the area and liked the townhouse development, as he and his wife had lived there during the early years of their marriage. With the Internet it was easy to look at choices and then travel there to look at five or six 'finalists'. At this point some of her four children, and local friends, thought she was crazy—she didn't fit the "code," rules, and conventions for her age, especially as a widow.

Then came the "sorting" or "*Shoebox*" step of reducing the volume of choices and throwing out negative evidence such as a second floor master bedroom or prices that were too high or too low and all foreclosures as they tended to be really messed up with equipment missing or not in working order. Also she knew the townhouse development she liked was near the beach and had two heated swimming pools, and good, reliable maintenance crews. She had learned also that one could buy a "turn-key" home that was almost completely furnished. From the Internet she found two of these that had furniture she liked and bid on them. One family did buy one of these and donated the furniture to charity. Both townhouses this writer had bid on were taken off the market immediately, as the owners hadn't realized that the current going prices (in 2011) were so low. Trying this "new adventure" allowed her to spend time researching new possibilities and alternatives plus consider financial and other issues. These were the 'Evidence' plus 'Interactions' steps in the Sensemaking Flow Chart.

Sensemaking and Schemas followed when she bid on an unfurnished townhouse with the exact floor plan she wanted, but at a somewhat lower price due to being unfurnished. This lower price allowed the difference between it and the price planned, to be used to purchase furniture—which was also on sale.

One of her hypotheses included having a 'room-delivery' store deliver furniture, but in checking *multiple sources* she chose a chain near her main home that she thought also had a store near the new location, but it was not the same. It was a different chain. A hefty delivery charge was involved—similar to a moving van charge for any home move, however. So in sorting through this hypothesis and generality she found additional items could be purchased online, that were on sale and offered 'free shipping' as a sales incentive. At this point she was "tweaking" her 'presentation' so that her children wouldn't think she was so 'crazy'.

As she settled in and stayed in the new place she came to realize that there were new "codes" and conventions for being there as an older or retired person. Many of this type of person were called "snowbirds" and were away half the year. Local utilities and services had 'seasonal rates' for part-time residents. Also she knew the codes and conventions were not required to be totally adopted—as the transition was *making sense*. (See Figure 2.2 in Chapter 2 for the "Knowledge Cycle".)

Presentation continued in settling in and furnishing the townhouse, as she found she really enjoyed it! It was easy to codify some activities and have more peers around with similar life stories and educational backgrounds and levels. As she "presented the story" and continued 'tweaking' she realized it was like preparing a PowerPoint presentation in the work place!

Conclusion

Story Book Version

Once upon a time the workplace was fairly routine in its tasks and expectations. Every day people did what was expected in expected ways and places. One day things changed. Information was available on the Internet and often too much information was presented to them and to children. Because of that people closed down and weren't willing to do new things. Because of that other people started sorting out what was old or relevant only to others, and having ideas to try out and to move forward.

Until finally we realized that transitions aren't some grim accommodation to modern life but are issues needing selection to two or three alternatives and testing, in order for us to learn new things via new avenues when local tradition and personal discretion are not enough. Sometimes this must be done several times. The best results for our workplaces, our lives, and our children require additional approaches in today's Information Age or Knowledge Era.

References

Bernard, S., (May 17, 2012) Speech given at AFFIRM luncheon, Sofitel Hotel, Washington, D.C.

Boisot, M. H. (1998). *Knowledge Assets: Securing Competitive Advantage in the Information Economy.* Oxford: Oxford University Press.

Gioia, D.A. and K. Chittipeddi (2001). Sensemaking, and Sensegiving in Strategic Change Initiation" in *Strategic Management Journal*, 12, 443-448, Sept. 1991.

Card, S. K. Mackinlay, J.D. & Schneiderman, B. (1999). *Information Visualization: Using Vision Think*, San Francisco: Morgan-Kaufmann.

Friedman, Thomas (2013). "Thoughts on Change," in *Forbes*, May 27, p. 120.

Gray, D. and T. VanderWal (2012). *The Connected Company*, Sebastopol, CA: O'Reilly Media.

Gesell, A. (1956). *Youth: The Years from Ten to Sixteen.* NY: Harper and Brothers.

Hanford, P. (1996). "Developing Director and Executive Competencies in Strategic Thinking," in Garratt., B. ed. *Developing Strategic Thought: Rediscovering the Art of Direction-Giving.* London: Harper-Collins, 1996, pp. 188-222.

Kahneman, D. (2011). *Thinking Fast and Slow*, New York: Farrar, Straus and Groux, N.Y.

Mintzberg, H. (1994). The Fall and Rise of Strategic Planning. *Harvard Business Review*, 72, 107.

Moore, Dale (2012). "Strategic Thinking", Talk given at Wiley Conference Center, October, California, MD.

Moss, M, (2001). "Sensemaking, Complexity and Organizational Knowledge," in *Knowledge and Process Management*, 8 (4), 217-232.

Pink, D. (2009). *DRIVE: The Surprising Truth about What Motivates Us*, N.Y.: Riverhead Books.

Pink, D. (2006). *A Whole New Mind: Why Right Brainers will Rule the Future,* Riverhead Books, N.Y.

Pirolli, P. and S. Card (1999) *"The Sensemaking Process and Leverage Points for Analyst Technology as Identified through Cognitive Task Analysis"* from the Advanced Research and Deveopment Activity, Novel Intelligence from the Massive Data Program.

Popper, R. (2008) Foresight Methodology, in Georghiou, L., Cassingena, J., Keenan, M., Miles, I. and Popper, R. (eds.), The Handbook of Technology Foresight, Edward Elgar, Cheltenham, pp. 44-88.

Thomas, J. B., Clark, S. M. and D.A. Gioia (1993). Strategic Sensemaking and Organizational Performance: Linkages Among Scanning, Interpretation and Outcomes, *The Academy of Management Journal, 36,* No. 2 Apr. 1993, pp. 239-270.

Uhl-Bien, Marion R. and Bill McKay (2007). Complexity Leadership Theory: Shifting Leadership from the Industrial Age to the Knowledge Era. *The Leadership Quarterly, 18,* 298-318.

Weick, K. E. (1995). *Sensemaking in Organizations.* Thousand Oaks: Sage.

Wheatley, Margaret, (1994) "New Ideas from the Army (Really)". *Fortune,* Sept. 19, 1994, pp. 135-139.

Wheatley, M. (1999, 2006). *Leadership and the New Science,* San Francisco, CA: Berrett-Koehler.

www.ingramcontent.com/pod-product-compliance
Lightning Source LLC
Chambersburg PA
CBHW021900170526
45157CB00005B/1901